To Valerie Eliot
who brought great happiness to a great poet
with love

CONTENTS

ACKNOWLEDGMENTS

SEVERAL PEOPLE, all of them more intelligent and learned than me, have read this short book and made shrewd suggestions, which I have acted on. I am very grateful to Mark Griffith, Adam Thirlwell, A. D. Nuttall, Julie Maxwell, Nina Raine, and my wife, Ann Pasternak Slater.

T. S. ELIOT WAS BORN IN ST LOUIS, MISSOURI, on 26 September 1888. He died in London aged seventy-seven. By then, he was the 1948 winner of the Nobel Prize for Literature and, in the same year, the recipient of the Order of Merit, England's most distinguished honour, in the personal gift of the reigning monarch. He was the most influential and authoritative literary arbiter of the twentieth century and a publisher of great distinction at Faber and Faber, where he published W. H. Auden, Louis MacNeice, and Stephen Spender. As the editor of the influential magazine *The Criterion*, from 1922 until 1939, he published Proust, Gide and Thomas Mann—an indication of his cultural pan-Europeanism as well as his access to the literary firmament. He was a world figure. Late in his career, he was a surprisingly successful poetic dramatist. He was the century's most famous poet— oddly, because his prestige was founded on poetry notorious for its difficulty. In 6 March 1950, he was on the cover of *Time* magazine. On 30 April 1956, Eliot lectured to fourteen thousand people at the baseball stadium in Minneapolis on 'The Frontiers of Criticism'. In Raymond Chandler's novel *The Long Goodbye* (1953), when Amos, the African-American chauffeur of Mrs. Loring, refuses a dollar tip, Philip Marlowe mildly twits his fastidiousness by offering to buy him the poems of T. S. Eliot; 'He said he already had them.' A hundred pages on, Marlowe and Amos have a plausible discussion—Amos is a graduate of Howard University—about 'The Love Song of J. Alfred Prufrock'. (They agree 'that the guy didn't know very much about women'.)

Eliot's detractors often insinuate that this eminence was achieved by feline caution, literary politicking, calculation, a shrewd assessment of the literary marketplace, a quiet but inexorable campaign of ruthless self-advancement. I think it is a matter of literary merit rather than manipulation of opinion. In fact, *Imagination of the Heart*, Theresa Whistler's biography of Walter de la Mare, demonstrates that 1922, the agreed date for the conclusive advent of modernism—with the publication of Joyce's *Ulysses*, Eliot's *The Waste Land*, and Wallace Stevens's *Harmonium*—seemed much less conclusive to de la Mare, J. C. Squire, and other tenacious neo-Georgians, 'also-rans' who had their own platforms including *The London Mercury* and the *Weekly Westminster*, to which the young Graham Greene contributed. It wasn't a question of capturing the sole radio station. The strategic battles were still being 'fought' in the 1950s. Walter de la Mare thought the selection of Eliot as the only twentieth-century English poet at the Festival of Britain in 1953 was invidious—and wrote to Eliot asking him to withdraw.

Despite this latter-day celebrity, for much of his life, Eliot's fame was restricted to literature. He was a private person. In his newspaper column, Gilbert Harding, a once-famous, now forgotten, British broadcasting celebrity, recounted his embarrassment at being pointed out on the London underground while Eliot, 'the greatest poet of the century', was ignored, unrecognised in the corner of the same compartment.

Eliot's life, like the lives of many writers who spend their time at their desks, was apparently uneventful compared to, say, Ernest Hemingway's blood-boltered, flashbulb-tormented exploits. In 'To Criticise the Critic' (1961), he described himself as 'the mild-mannered man safely entrenched behind his typewriter'. And it is a theme of this study that the Buried Life, the idea of a life not fully lived, is the central, animating idea of Eliot's poetry.

However, Eliot's own life is full of quiet drama, even of recklessness.

On the one hand, there is the assiduous man of letters, indefatigably reviewing, editing, and giving lectures. On the other hand, there is the poet who renounced a promising career as a philosopher in American academe for an uncertain literary life in a foreign country, the poet who married, within weeks of meeting her, Vivien Haigh-Wood. Though initially Vivien was a valued, even essential literary confrere and a loved wife—'I have felt happier, these few days, than ever in my life', Eliot writes to Bertrand Russell on 14 January 1916—the marriage was not a success. On 10 January 1916, Eliot writes to Conrad Aiken that financial worries and concern over Vivien's poor health had stopped him writing: Yet, 'I am having a wonderful time nevertheless. I have *lived* through material for a score of long poems in the last six months. An entirely different life from that I looked forward to two years ago. Cambridge [Mass.] seems to me a dull nightmare now . . . '. Vivien committed adultery with Bertrand Russell, Eliot's ex-teacher and mentor. Eliot was legally separated from her in 1933. Gradually, she went mad and in 1938 was committed by her brother Maurice. She died in a private mental hospital in Finsbury Park, London, on 23 January 1947.

In June 1927, Eliot was received into the Church of England, and in November became a naturalised British citizen. Virginia Woolf writes of Eliot 'in his four piece suit'—repressed, reserved, buttoned-up. If we concentrate too much on the Lloyds banker in his pin-striped trousers, the London publisher with his bowler hat and rolled umbrella, and Eliot's own ironic self-portrait as the circumspect pedant—'Restricted to What Precisely / And If and Perhaps and But'—we are likely to overlook the man whose religious conversion first announced itself in the Vatican when Eliot fell to his knees in front of Michelangelo's *Pietà* to the amazement of his brother Henry Ware Eliot. Eliot isn't the dry stick of his self-caricature. This is Robert Lowell describing Eliot dancing with Valerie, his new bride and second wife, forty years younger than himself, and married in secret at the age of sixty-nine: 'they danced so dashingly at the Charles River boatclub brawl that he was called "Elbows Eliot".'

Given that the main events of Eliot's life are so sensational, even lurid, it may seem odd that the central focus of his oeuvre should concentrate on the life not fully lived, 'buried', avoided, sidestepped. It is conceivable, though, that these dramatic decisions in Eliot's life were provoked by the very fear of not living fully—of opting for insurance rather than risk. The theme itself comes from literature, not 'life'—from Henry James in the first instance, but fed by the main current of nineteenth-century literature. We writers frequently inherit our themes from our most admired predecessors. It is they who set the agenda. It is we who continue it, who develop it. It is important to realize that, for writers, the fully lived life also means the interior life, the mental life. Grey matter acting on reading matter is a matter of passion, too.

This contradiction—between the risks Eliot took in his own life and his dominant theme of debilitating caution—makes it difficult to equate biographical events with the poetry. Unlike Sylvia Plath—whose poetry cannot be understood without the prior knowledge that her marriage to Ted Hughes failed and that she was a suicide risk—Eliot's poetry is committed to impersonality. The life hardly helps us at all as readers. In 'The Frontiers of Criticism' (1961), Eliot lays out this position:

> For myself, I can only say that a knowledge of the springs that released a poem is not necessarily a help towards understanding the poem: too much information about the origins of the poem may even break my contact with it. I feel no need for any light upon [Wordsworth's] Lucy poems beyond the radiance shed by the poems themselves.

It is possible to see this as evasive. Many recent commentators have done so. They prefer a guilty poet trying to deny responsibility for a mad wife; a bisexual philanderer; an ambitious, reptilian anti-Semite who was prepared to pimp his wife to other men in order to advance his literary career. There is no evidence that Eliot was either a fornicator or a homosexual. These are the flimsy insinuations of the unscrupulous and unscholarly biographer. Eliot never repudiated his first wife. Until she was committed by her brother, Eliot made sure she was watched over by mutual friends. He could not live with her, however. In the light of her extraordinary behavior, his decision is reasonable—route marches through London in full Fascist uniform looking for him, well-and-widely-attested paranoia, pushing chocolate through the Faber letter-box. The idea that Eliot pimped Vivien to Russell is pure malicious supposition. If anything, the evidence suggests that Eliot, like many another cuckold, found out much later. Nor is his alleged anti-Semitism a simple matter of record—as I hope to show.

The usual links between the life and the art are problematic in Eliot's case because he held a theory about the impersonality of great art—outlined in his essay 'Tradition and the Individual Talent' (1919). I discuss this in chapter 6, but let me anticipate a little here. Essentially, the author of *Ash-Wednesday* ('Because I do not hope . . .') can hardly have meant to rule out the personal. Eliot's 'impersonality' addresses and describes the artistic process, the artistic *treatment* of the personal.

Eliot's essay was classicist, an aesthetic whose thrust was essentially negative, defined in opposition to romanticism. The romantic position values strong emotions, makes them central to the achievement of art. It was a mistake Eliot was determined to overturn: in art, he wrote, 'it is not the "greatness", the intensity, of the emotions, the components, but the intensity of the artistic process, the pressure, so to speak, under which the fusion takes place, that counts.' Instead, he argued for the impersonality of great art. By 'impersonality' Eliot meant objectivity, impartiality, disinterestedness, distance—the control of accidentals, of subjectivity, of mere contingencies. Hence the idea of the objective correlative and its implied contract between writer and reader—that the impenetrably private is inadmissible as art.

But this does not mean, could not mean, that art should be purged of anything personal—as many have wrongly believed. On the contrary, Eliot maintains the emotions are what we make art from. Look at that quotation again: 'it is not the "greatness", the intensity, of the emotions, *the components* [my italics] . . .' The emotions are 'the components', but they have to be made into something. 'Tradition and the Individual Talent' *is*, though, a denunciation of unreconstructed subjectivity in art. Strong feelings cannot make you a poet. Otherwise, every sentimental drunk, every football fan, every religious bigot would qualify. Creativity means creating something.

Nevertheless, aesthetic distance means that it is dangerous and difficult to translate the poetry, to 'money-change' the poetry, back into personal experience. For instance, I was once asked on a television film if Eliot was Prufrock in 'The Love Song of J. Alfred Prufrock'. I explained that Eliot was cultured, whereas Prufrock was intimidated by the idea of talking about Michelangelo; that Eliot came from good family and was unlikely to be thrown socially by the presence of a footman. I argued that, whereas Eliot was the palpably passionate author of the line 'blood shaking my heart / The awful daring of a moment's surrender', the character Prufrock was as 'uptight as a rolled umbrella'—a sound bite which was followed in the film's final edit by a photograph of Eliot outside the doors of Faber and Gwyer, leaning on a rolled umbrella. Rhetorical editing of perverse genius that was a thousand miles from my intention—or the truth about Eliot, who married Vivien without first telling his parents.

There aren't any easy equations. Gerontion is a character in a dramatic monologue, not a transparent disguise for the poet.

In the end, we are left with the poetry. It speaks to any attentive reader. An accountant I know read *The Waste Land* and picked out two words from the passage in which the neurotic woman brushes her hair: 'her hair / Spread out in fiery points / Glowed into words, then would be *savagely still* [my italics]'. The unusual, counterintuitive combination of savagery and stillness impressed him. He was right to be impressed, to feel a frisson of repressed rage in the tense paradox. It is for these verbal gifts that we read Eliot's poetry. This is the light, the radiance cast by the poetry itself.

Introduction

———

ELIOT AND THE
BURIED LIFE

IN HIS ESSAY 'JOHN FORD', Eliot says that 'the whole of Shakespeare's work is *one* poem'. He continues, 'and it is the poetry of it in this sense, not the poetry of isolated lines and passages or the poetry of single figures which he created, that matters most.' Eliot maintains that it is this 'one significant, consistent and developing personality', that makes Shakespeare 'a great poet'. And yet, though he identifies the presence of this 'personality', he does not analyse its constituents. In this study of Eliot, I have attempted to characterise *his* 'significant, consistent and developing personality'. I want, in the words of Matthew Arnold, to see his achievement 'steadily and see it whole'. But I have also tried to do local justice to Eliot's genius at the level of the word, the phrase, and the passage. I am interested in the '*one* poem', but it would be philistine to slight the detail of individual poems.

Eliot's lifelong themes, despite the manifest and exemplary variety of the poems, are consistent. One major theme is the failure to live fully. Eliot inherits this theme, the theme of the 'buried life', from his awkward critical and poetic father figure, Matthew Arnold. Arnold formulated the idea of the 'buried life'. For Arnold, the buried life describes our failure to realise our emotional potential—essentially because the *business* of living supplants the cultivation of the inner life. (Oscar Wilde, Arnold's unlikely disciple, was to advocate the intensive cultivation of individuality in 'The Soul of Man under Socialism'.) But Arnold adds the refinement that the problem is not simply one of frustration: ignorance of what we really feel, lack of true self-awareness, means that we are mysteries to ourselves, and therefore find fulfilment difficult or impossible.

At the same time, Eliot is also a modernist, with a commitment to a classicist position. He is, therefore, sceptical about emotion, about strong emotion, as an obvious good in itself. His poetry is a scrupulous record of human emotions, sifting what we feel from what we think we *ought* to feel. Eliot has an eye and an ear for the fake.

Potentially, there is a conflict between these two fundamental impulses—one of which wishes to maximise emotion, the other of which is sceptical of emotion and scathing about sentimentality. My first two chapters analyse each impulse in turn before reconciling them at the end of chapter 2.

Almost a motif in this book, the idea of the buried life is one that underlies much of Eliot's work in many different ways—it is inherited, then explored and mined by Eliot in ways that expand Arnold's original analysis. To the rationed heart and to self-ignorance, Eliot adds other occluded selves—our hidden motives; our previous incarnations; our nonrational, unconscious mystical experiences; the previous lives of literature and of words themselves; the continuing life within us of dead ancestors; and the power of the irrational.

The buried life in Eliot has a headstone with many names, different names for a familiar compound ghost.

One

THE FAILURE TO LIVE

'But most people are only very little alive'

T. S. Eliot, *After Strange Gods*

WHEN ELIOT MARRIED VIVIEN HAIGH-WOOD, he wrote to his brother, Henry Ware Eliot, on 2 July 1915: 'I feel more alive than I ever have before'. I think that contradicts Bertrand Russell, who said of his former pupil's marriage: 'he is exquisite and listless; she says she married him in order to stimulate him, but finds she can't do it'. On the other hand, 'more alive' is comparative. The phrase does not necessarily mean that Eliot was 'breathing fire and ozone'—merely that he was more alive than formerly.

It was Ezra Pound, in a letter to Harriet Monroe, the editor of *Poetry*, dated 31 January 1915, who said of Prufrock, the protagonist of 'The Love Song of J. Alfred Prufrock' (June 1915): 'a portrait satire on futility can't end by turning that quintessence of futility, Mr P into a reformed character breathing out fire and ozone'. It would be foolish to identify Eliot with his creations, but

Prufrock's failure to seize the day, his resolve to remain repressed, avoiding the element of risk that is part of truly living, is something Eliot was to return to—obsessively but covertly.

Ten years after 'Prufrock', in *The Waste Land*, Eliot again touches on this idea: 'Are you alive, or not?' asks the hysterical woman of 'A Game of Chess'. I don't mean to identify her with Vivien. I want merely to suggest that the failure to live fully is a central, recurring theme of Eliot's poetry.

It is the figure in his carpet.

In 1929, it is the subject of the Ariel poem, 'Animula'[1]. Here, Eliot depicts a psychically damaged, confined soul corroded by its own caution, a life disfigured and distorted, rusty with reluctance.

'Animula' isn't a much-noted poem, but it is quietly central and you can clearly see how it is related to an earlier, greater poem, *The Waste Land* (1922). Both poems share a topos—of death as accumulated documentation, the paper detritus we leave behind. Their poetic economies overlap. *The Waste Land*'s 'blood shaking my heart' in 'Animula' becomes 'the importunity of the blood'. And *The Waste Land*'s 'lean solicitor' breaking the seals on documents becomes 'Leaving disordered papers in a dusty room'.

"Issues from the hand of God, the simple soul": the poem begins with a line concocted from Dante's *Purgatorio* (XVI) that describes Marco Lombardo and is quoted in Eliot's essay on Dante. In Eliot's poem, however, the subject, the 'little soul' of the title, is appropriately nameless because the individual has in effect refused to encounter the forces that shape us as individuals—and yet has inevitably been uniquely misshapen. Eliot reprises and varies his opening line from Dante:

Issues from the hand of time the simple soul
Irresolute and selfish, misshapen, lame,

Unable to fare forward or retreat,

Fearing the warm reality, the offered good,

Denying the importunity of the blood

Eliot, brilliantly, is careful not to overstate the case. The subject is no Dorian Gray, outwardly beautiful but actually hideously disfigured by his immoral life. Eliot eschews melodrama. Nothing actively evil has taken place. The subject is 'selfish', an adjective whose modesty is genius—not a grandiose sin like cruelty or murder or even fornication. An opportunity has been missed—the opportunity to live fully.

The poignancy of this failure—its human poverty—is underlined by Eliot's rich, detailed evocation of childhood. Of course, he cannot match the bravura of Joyce: 'When you wet the bed first it is warm then it gets cold. His mother put on the oilsheet. That had a queer smell.' But in its own way, 'Animula' reproduces childhood's typically olfactory vividness: 'the *fragrant* [my italics] brilliance of the Christmas tree'. And he is true to its occlusions and surprises, its innocence shading into naivety: 'Content with . . . What the fairies do and what the servants say.' The initial childish confidence plausibly coexists with childish wariness. It takes a good poet to suggest both a recurrent action and a calculating, cautious temperament in the verb 'studies'—'Studies the sunlit pattern on the floor / And running stags around a silver tray'. Everyone's early life is lived in close-up and curiosity, so these details are both particular and generic. But the verb 'studies', is at once typical and inflected. It is the ailing seed of the future. It goes with the child who curls up with the *Encyclopaedia Britannica*.

This quietly rich notation is marred briefly by one line of mechanical verbal oppositions: 'To light, dark, dry or damp, chilly or warm'. (The mechanical chiasmus of 'Perplexes and offends more, day by day; / Week by week, offends and perplexes more' is another local failure.)

Eliot's fine, bold strategy in 'Animula' is to take his reader from this minutely informed beginning to the moment of death. Entirely and appropriately omitting the life—an excluded middle that hasn't been lived:

> Leaving disordered papers in a dusty room;
> Living first in the silence after the viaticum.

The viaticum is the Eucharist given to persons in danger of death. There is something Beckettian here—something reminiscent of Krapp's perpetual postponement of life for the arid embrace of art. There is bitter pathos in the realisation that intense life should be brought into being only by the knowledge of its imminent extinction—'Living *first* . . .'.

Then Eliot evokes incautious, adventurous figures who *have* lived, and lived dangerously: Guiterriez 'avid of speed and power', 'Boudin, blown to pieces', 'Floret, by the boarhound slain'. Whereas, the 'simple soul' was effectively dead and only began to live in the brief interlude before death—'in the silence after the viaticum'. Significantly, though Guiterriez, Boudin, and (the somehow fifteenth-century) Floret are invented figures, they are given names and identities, in contrast to the nameless subject with his fragile ontology.

Effectively, Eliot inverts the expectations of the traditional debate between the active and the contemplative life—where the bias is in favour of the contemplative life, as, for instance, in Marvell's 'The Garden'. Eliot subverts the cliché—not for the last time. It may seem perverse of him to promote the reckless—Boudin,

Guiterriez—and demote the prudent, but Eliot believed it was 'better to do evil . . . than to do nothing', as he paradoxically avowed in his 1930 essay on Baudelaire.

Just as the end of 'Animula' summons the reckless spirits of Guiterriez and Boudin, the beginning of 'Gerontion'—another poem about the failure to live—invokes the idea of Thermopylae: 'I was neither at the hot gates', the hot gates where Leonidas and his small band of Spartans held back an army.

And Eliot's purpose is the same—to contrast the brave with the psychically torpid. (The contrast is repeated for a third time in *The Hollow Men*, where the 'lost, violent souls' are set against the flimsy, spectral hollow men—becoming an Eliotean argumentative trope.) The syntax of the opening of 'Gerontion' deliberately calls up the epic with its pastiche Latinate syntax, which postpones the last main verb to the end:

Here I am, an old man in a dry month,
Being read to by a boy, waiting for rain.
I was neither at the hot gates
Nor fought in the warm rain
Nor knee deep in the salt marsh, heaving a cutlass,
Bitten by flies, fought.

Of course, in these lines we are made party to what is being read— as it might be, Herodotus—by the boy to the little old man who is the speaker. The lines have the force of *occultatio*—the figure of speech which, by denying something actually draws attention to it. For a series of non-events, the lines are action packed—we expect 'cold rain', but 'warm rain' avoids the anticipated contrast with 'hot gates' and drenches the reader in particularity. The same is true of the specifics of the salt marsh. Nevertheless, plunged in the moment though we are, Eliot carefully preserves the linguistic awkwardness, the deferred main verb 'fought' that tells us the events are written—and at a remove, therefore, from real experience.[2]

'Bitten by flies, fought'. Not for the last time, Eliot subtly mixes his messages. He leads us through difficult terrain—that 'salt marsh'—only to rescind the illusion of action conclusively with that bookishly placed final verb. It is a procedure perfect for Eliot's purpose—the portrayal of a psychic wallflower, a noncombatant, an over-conscientious objector, a constitutional abstainer.

In contrast to Leonidas and the Hoplites at Thermopylae, these are the sensational tabloid headlines of Gerontion's actual existence: 'The goat coughs at night in the field overhead'; 'The woman . . . sneezes at evening'. It's not even a flu epidemic. *Waiting for Godot* was famously described as a play in which nothing happens—twice. 'Gerontion' is a poem spoken by a voluptuary of inaction with an extensive collection of alibis. It is about the failure to live, spiritually or physically. Eliot was always interested in self-justification, our refusal to think badly of ourselves: 'nothing dies harder than the desire to think well of oneself', he writes in 'Shakespeare and the Stoicism of Seneca' (1927). As Nietzsche ruefully notes in *Beyond Good and Evil*: '"I have done that," says my memory. "I cannot have done that"—says my pride, and remains adamant. At last—memory yields.' It is no accident that Eliot cites Nietzsche three times in this essay, crediting him with the culmination of a Senecan tendency—an acute awareness of self-dramatisation. This isn't particular to Eliot, his own secret flaw. It is common to every one of us.

Gerontion's excuse is life's inherent inconsequentiality, the disjunction between cause and effect; if *a*, then not necessarily *b*. This first alibi can be summarised by quoting Eliot's 'Portrait of a Lady':

'(But our beginnings never know our ends!).' 'Gerontion' goes on to 'analyse' this discontinuity in broad terms but begins with a specific example. Those who want a sign, an omen, are presented with the infant Christ—a sign that is taken for a wonder although the child is swaddled and 'unable to speak a word'. The sign, then, is opaque, enigmatic, and, in Gerontion's version, wrong. The expected result of the infant Christ—an infancy associated, reasonably enough, with innocence and gentleness—is overridden, superseded. 'In the juvescence of the year / Came Christ the tiger'. The tiger is, I take it, a figure for the appalling collateral, the fallout of religion—martyrs, crusades, schism, Inquisition, disembowelling, branding, beheading, and torture.

Gerontion's major justification for doing nothing is the famous passage beginning 'After such knowledge, what forgiveness?'(ll 33–47) whose sinuous argument personifies History as perverse and contrarian. In the second of his *Meditations on First Philosophy*, Descartes proposes the hypothesis that the universe is ruled by an Arch-Deceiver, whose purpose is to mislead mankind at every turn. Gerontion's female History is very similar. She kindles the wrong motives—ambition and vanity. She realises our ambitions when our attention is elsewhere and has moved on. Or when we no longer want the thing we once wanted. We achieve our aims too soon, too late, confusingly, in ways which so exceed the initial desire that we are sated. Our best motives produce the worst outcomes. Crimes are the cause of virtue. In this account, History isn't a lottery. It is *consistently* perverse.

> After such knowledge, what forgiveness? Think now
> History has many cunning passages, contrived corridors
> And issues, deceives with whispering ambitions,

Guides us by vanities. Think now
She gives when our attention is distracted
And what she gives, gives with such supple confusions
That the giving famishes the craving. Gives too late
What's not believed in, or if still believed,
In memory only, reconsidered passion. Gives too soon
Into weak hands, what's thought can be dispensed with
Till the refusal propagates a fear. Think
Neither fear nor courage saves us. Unnatural vices
Are fathered by our heroism. Virtues
Are forced upon us by our impudent crimes.

It is a superb paragraph. Arranged very clearly around the repeated imperative, 'Think now', it ends with two symmetrical paradoxes—'Unnatural vices / Are fathered by our heroism. Virtues / Are forced upon us by our impudent crimes'. Despite the illusion of clarity in the arrangement of those imperatives, the exposition as a whole brilliantly enacts the 'supple confusions' it attributes to History. Smoke, mirrors, backlighting, with the aim not of enlightening the reader, but bamboozling him—and acquitting the speaker of cowardice by supplying a maze of motives. The slippery heart of the paragraph is difficult to paraphrase accurately as it qualifies its qualifications: '[History] Gives too late / What's not believed in, or if still believed, / In memory only, reconsidered passion.' Not impossible to understand, it's true; unlike 'Gives too soon / Into weak hands, what's thought can be dispensed with / Till the refusal propagates a fear.' Eh? We need to know what's *what* in 'what's thought can be dispensed with' or the sentence is opaque. And the 'what' is withheld.

The statement is clarified only if we introduce an extra verb: 'Gives too soon / Into weak hands, [gives] what's thought can be dispensed with / Till the refusal propagates a fear.' Instead of one enigmatic pronouncement, we now have two clearer statements.

In the midst of these carefully abstract propositions advanced by Gerontion to explain his failure to live, we can hear two words that suggest he is skirting more personal matter—'craving', 'passion'. 'That the giving famishes the *craving*. Gives too late / What's not believed in, or if still believed, / In memory only, reconsidered *passion*' [my italics]. And so it proves: 'I that was near your heart was removed therefrom.' The pedantry of 'therefrom'—its tiny cough in ink—is a perfect touch of characterisation.

Who is Gerontion addressing? Whose heart was he once near? She is unnamed, in a poem that otherwise uses proper names brilliantly. No writer, not Marlowe, not even Milton, has used names to better effect than Eliot in 'Gerontion'—Hakagawa, Madame de Tornquist, Mr. Silvero, Mrs. Cammel, Fräulein von Kulp—poised between the exotic and the utterly particular, perfectly judged. People whose individuality and presence is all in their names. Whose dark biographies are there in a gesture—'shifting the candles', 'one hand on the door', or Hakagawa apparently bowing in homage, but actually bending to read the museum labels. These figures are conducting a séance, taking part in a parodic communion: 'flowering judas, / To be eaten, to be divided, to be drunk / Among whispers.' Gerontion, though, has 'no ghosts'. He is neither spiritual, nor a Spiritualist.

'I that was near your heart was removed therefrom / To lose beauty in terror, terror in inquisition.' The second line is baffling. Let us quickly eliminate one difficulty—the Inquisition. We associate the Inquisition with terror, whereas here it appears to be an *antidote* to terror. Conceivably, the greater terror consumes the lesser terror. But, in fact, the Inquisition is irrelevant.[3] The sense of the line is this: I lost your beauty because I was terrified by it, and afterwards this terror evaporated as I questioned myself endlessly about it. In other words, the timorous Gerontion was terrified ('terror') and then fertile with mental scruples ('inquisition') so the original impulse was talked to death. I am reminded of A. H. Clough's 'Dipsychus'. Clough, the friend of Matthew Arnold, is often misrepresented as a poet of comparably high Victorian seriousness, but he has a grave levity, a modest irony that is modernist *avant la lettre*. Dipsychus, the shilly-shallier, puts love to death with an overdose of meticulously punctuated qualifications:

> But love, the large repose
> Restorative, not to mere outside needs
> Skin-deep, but thoroughly to the total man,
> Exists, I will believe, but so, so rare,
> So doubtful, so exceptional, hard to guess;
> When guessed, so often counterfeit; in brief,
> A thing not possibly to be conceived
> An item in the reckonings of the wise.

In tone and attack, this is not unlike Eliot's 'After such knowledge' passage—fussier, shorn of eloquence, but reminiscent. 'When guessed, so often counterfeit.'

Why is Gerontion telling us his tale of unsuccessful love? Because the woman he once failed to love is dead: 'I have lost my sight, smell, hearing, taste and touch: / How should I use them for your closer contact?' And if he can summon her dead presence, it isn't by means of a séance: 'it is not by any concitation [distur-bance, agitation, excitement, rousing, conjuring] / Of the back-ward devils.' Their 'relationship', such as it is, such as it was, continues after her death, and, Gerontion imagines, after his own death: 'Think at last / We have not reached conclusion, when I / Stiffen in a rented house.' It is not, I think, because Gerontion believes in life after death. After all, De Bailhache, Fresca, and Mrs. Cammel are so many 'fractured atoms', 'whirled / Beyond the circuit of the shuddering Bear'.[4] It is because Gerontion's view of extinction is, like the 'proof' of Zeno's Paradox, one of infinite gradualism, 'a thousand small deliberations'. Like the old joke about the death of the Master of Magdalen: 'How can you tell?'

And that is all we know about this un-couple, who are like Crusoe's 'two shoes that were not fellows'—unless we accept the allusion to Henry James's short story, 'The Beast in the Jungle', in the line: 'The tiger springs in the new year. Us he devours.'[5]

The James story is about John Marcher, a man who feels marked out by destiny, 'the sense of being kept for something rare and strange, possibly prodigious and terrible'—which will thus dis-tinguish him from everyone else. His image for this event, what-ever it impends, is a beast in the jungle, waiting to spring. He confides his sense of destiny to May Bartram, who shares his sus-pense. He discounts the possibility of marrying: 'a man of feeling didn't cause himself to be accompanied by a lady on a tiger-hunt'. A year after May Bartram dies, Marcher finally realises that the unique thing that is to happen to him is that *nothing* is to happen to him. It is a classic Jamesian ironic inversion. Whereupon Marcher realises that, in his egotism and self-regard, he has failed to see what May should have meant to him: 'The escape would have been to love her; then, *then* he would have lived. *She* had lived—who could say now with what passion?—since she had loved him for himself; whereas he had never thought of her (ah, how it hugely glared at him!) but in the chill of his egotism and the light of her use.'

Marcher's chill egotism and Gerontion's disabling terror are not an exact match, but they share the failure to live with 'Animula': '*then he would have lived*.' And in this regret, Eliot and James are part of a tradition—the familiar romantic idea that life is to be lived to the full. It is most passionately and intelligently put in Lambert Strether's instruction to Little Bilham in *The Ambassadors*: 'Live, live all you can. It's a mistake not to.'

But the idea is a staple of nineteenth-century fiction, where it is both ironised and advocated—an ambivalence shared by Eliot. On the one hand, there is Pater's advocacy, his sense that life is 'a short day of frost and sun' and that success in life is therefore to burn with a 'hard gemlike flame'.[6]

On the other hand, you could regard this counselled intensity as merely the glamorised version of a nebulous, sentimental discontent with the unexciting realities of life. Emma Bovary, trapped in mediocrity, is like Marcher: 'And all the time, deep within her, she was waiting for something to happen.' Like Gerontion watching the woman 'poking the peevish gutter', Emma's life has atrophied: 'So she sat there holding the tongs in the fire or watching the rain fall.' But she is ironised by Flaubert for demanding more from life than it can offer—for attending to the unreasonable imperatives of romantic fiction.

Chekhov's stories, too, are thronged with ironised romantics whose cry is 'I want to live'—a desire identically expressed by Kleopatra in 'My Life', by the consumptive narrator of 'An Anonymous Story', by Anna Sergeyevna in 'The Lady with the Little

Dog'. These, and many others, are sick with the suspicion that life has more intense emotion to offer than they are experiencing. So, too, in opera—the famous aria in Gounod's *Roméo et Juliette*, 'Ah! Je veux vivre!'

Those too timid, or too frigid (like Joyce's Mr. Duffy), to partake of 'life's feast', to *live*, are roundly mocked in 'Whispers of Immortality'. This poem in quatrains was first published in September 1918 in the *Little Review*. It turns on the contrast between the Elizabethans and Eliot's contemporaries, between the fraught and the merely febrile. It is about facing up to mortality, the only end of flesh, and the modern sexual fear of flesh. On the one hand, Eliot presents us with Webster and Donne. Both are genuinely haunted by death. Flesh, even when desirable, is a reminder to both of mortality. The two differ, however. Webster uses bodily corruption for sexual arousal: '[Webster] knew that thought clings round dead limbs / Tightening its lusts and luxuries.' Donne's sex is devoid of tenderness, even the merest inflection: 'To seize and clutch and penetrate.' The verbs are unqualified, desolate. (And there is a bleak, concealed irony in the apparent tautology of 'seize' and 'clutch'. As we differentiate, we see from the sequence that 'clutch' is intended as a brutish approximation of 'embrace' or 'stroke'.)

Eliot's contrast is between the Elizabethan writers and modern man, who is intimidated by flesh, too—but for a different reason. In the second half of 'Whispers of Immortality', Eliot introduces a Russian female, Grishkin, whose magnificent animality, whose *powerful* physical presence, is vital—and therefore intimidating. Yet her sex appeal is without calculation, without consciousness. It is *unaware*, simple, shorn of complication—and a million miles from serving as a reminder of mortality. Some critics have seen evidence of misogyny in Eliot's catalogue of Grishkin's physical attributes—particularly the references to her bodily odours: 'so rank a feline smell.' But she isn't the predatory man-eater of popular cliché. I think these critics are deaf to the gentle accumulation of comic attributes in Eliot's portrait. It begins by stressing Grishkin's undesigning innocence: 'Grishkin is nice.' This is a property that coexists with her powerful sexuality and her other property, the 'maisonnette' she lives in. Eliot's method is affectionate zeugma, juxtaposing the carnal and the innocently inconsequential.

Finally, her concrete force is such that abstract ideas take evasive action: they 'circumambulate her charm'. But the joke is not on Grishkin. The real joke is on the timid men, 'our lot'[7]—as opposed to Webster and Donne. For us, death—bones, the 'dry ribs'—is a cosy refuge from discomfiting Grishkin.

The *locus classicus* of timidity in Eliot's poetry is *The Hollow Men* (1925), the first (radically different) thing Eliot wrote after *The Waste Land*. It is spoken by men without substance—without guts, without integrity—men who are spiritually gelded. But for this poem we need a different word. 'Timidity' isn't sufficiently grave. Eliot is here considering spiritual evasiveness—the torpid version of renunciation. His epigraph refers us to Conrad's *Heart of Darkness* and Mr. Kurtz. And hollowness features in Conrad's novella: 'I let him [the brickmaker of the Central Station] run on, this papier-maché Mephistopheles, and it seemed to me that if I tried I could poke my fore-finger through him, and would find nothing inside but a little loose dirt, maybe.' But *The Hollow Men* is a poem almost buried alive under the weight of commentary. Commonly we are invited to read it through the spectacles of books and history—*Heart of Darkness*, *Julius Caesar*, all three parts of Dante's *Divine Comedy* and Robert Catesby, Guy Fawkes and the Gunpowder Plot. None of these suggestions is stupid. But *The Hollow Men*, approached more directly, is a simple poem. Its simplicity, its broad clarity, seems to have baffled commentators geared up to read Eliot's poetry as if they were code crackers at Bletchley Park faced by Enigma.

The Hollow Men is set in Limbo, 'death's dream kingdom', 'the twilight kingdom'. It is spoken in the first person plural by men whose lives on Earth have been void, put to death by prudence—and whose after-existence, neither damned nor saved, is not an afterlife, but rather a contemptibly prolonged disengagement with the 'dangers' of human contact.

In the induction to Ben Jonson's *The Magnetic Lady*, a Boy addresses the audience: 'a good play is like a skein of silk; which if you take by the right end, you may wind off at pleasure, on the bottom or card of your discourse, in a tale or so; how you will: but if you light on the wrong end, you will pull all into a knot or elf-lock; which nothing but the shear, or a candle, will undo or separate.' So far, criticism of *The Hollow Men* has produced a tangle like a tarantula.

The 'right end', the one literary reference we need to know, is to Dante's *Inferno* canto 3 and its description of Limbo. Without it, the poem doesn't make sense. That is why Eliot takes unprecedented pains to lodge it in our minds in his essay 'What Dante Means to Me' (1950). He had already alluded to *Inferno* canto 3 in *The Waste Land*. For all his wry disclaimers about the notorious *Waste Land* notes, particularly in 'The Frontiers of Criticism' (1956), Eliot singles out this reference to Dante for special attention:

Readers of my *Waste Land* will perhaps remember that the vision of my city clerks trooping over London Bridge from the railway station to their offices evoked the reflection 'I had not thought death had undone so many'; and that in another place I deliberately modified a line of Dante by altering it—'sighs, short and infrequent, were exhaled'. And I gave the references in my notes, in order to make the reader who recognised the allusion, know that I meant him to recognise it, and *know that he would have missed the point if he did not recognise it.* [my italics]

The references are to *Inferno* canto III, lines 55–57 and to canto IV, lines 25–27. These two cantos describe not Hell proper, but the anteroom to Hell—which is Limbo. Many inhabitants of Limbo are beside Eliot's point—the virtuous but unbaptised, the great pagan poets (Homer, Lucan, Horace, and, of course, Dante's guide, Virgil), the great pagan philosophers (Zeno, Thales, Anaxagoras) and a *Who's Who* of pagan grandees, heroes, and heroines, including Caesar and Electra. These categories do not concern us.

Limbo also contains 'Questi sciaurati, che mai non fur vivi'— in Laurence Binyon's translation, 'These paltry, who *never were alive* [my italics]'.

This category *does* concern us—since the failure to live is a central Eliotean concern. These 'paltry' are rejected by Heaven and Hell alike—'a Dio spiacenti ed a' nemici sui.' [Odious to God and to his enemies.] [8] This group has 'spent / Life without infamy and without praise'. (They intermingle with the cowardly angels who fought neither for God nor Satan.) And it is this group which is described by Eliot's line, 'I had not thought death had undone so many'. Applied to the clerks in *The Waste Land*, the line doesn't mean that the living are actually dead. It means—a crucial, subtle shift of emphasis—that they are not fully alive.

The Hollow Men is set in Dante's Limbo and the Hollow Men are those who are rejected alike by heaven and hell because they have neither sinned nor been actively virtuous. They have abstained. They have failed to live. They are depleted, unvital: 'Shape without form, shade without colour, / Paralysed force, gesture without motion.' In contrast, there are the 'lost / Violent souls', sinners who have gone to Hell proper, 'death's other Kingdom'. They could include the Gunpowder Plot conspirators, but Eliot doesn't actually limit his broad category. (It could include Guiterriez, Boudin and Floret—sinners for whom Eliot asks us to pray at the end of 'Animula'.) The opening invokes the Guy Fawkes dummy—a thing without substance, stuffed with straw. This is the guy you burn on bonfires every 5 November—an effigy, not the real thing; a pseudo-Hell for a pseudo-person. This is a bold, even obvious symbol, much like Eliot's use of the waste land to adumbrate an arid spiritual condition.

At the end of the second section of his 1930 essay on Baudelaire, Eliot formulates an idea of the human that has shocked many liberal readers, but which throws light on *The Hollow Men* and which is explained in its turn by Eliot's poem: 'So far as we are human, what we do must either be evil or good; so far as we do evil or good, we are human; and it is better, in a paradoxical way, to do evil than to do nothing: at least, we exist.'

It is that penultimate clause we find unacceptable: how can it be true that it is better to do evil than do nothing? We immediately introduce incontrovertible examples. Is it better to kill a child than to ignore that child? Obviously not. Equally obviously, therefore, this cannot be what Eliot means—unless he has suffered a mental lapse. To understand him, we have, I think, to interpret less literally. We have to consider the fundamental polarity proposed by Eliot. It is between a theological view of the world, in which every action is significant and carries moral consequence, and a humanist view of the world, in which every action is drained of significance because there is neither salvation nor damnation, neither a heaven nor a hell, only moral opinion. On the one hand, good, evil, and eternal judgement; on the other hand, weightless actions, moral relativity, and the sense that nothing really matters ultimately.[9]

How is this relevant to Eliot's poem? *The Hollow Men* is an attack not on the active commission of sins, but on negativity—an unlife unlived, a kind of dishonesty, an existential *mauvaise foi*. Eliot thinks a life saturated in dangerous, even fatal, significance is preferable to one fundamentally without meaning: 'At least, we exist.'

Section II uses two slightly different epithets to describe Limbo. Since Limbo isn't Hell proper, it is 'death's dream kingdom' *and* 'the twilight kingdom'. *They are the same thing*—twilight being an intermediate stage between afternoon and darkness proper, just as Limbo is between death and Hell proper.

In this Limbo, evasion is the medium in which the speaker exists; it is the oxygen breathed by 'These paltry who never were alive'.

The speaker is relieved of human contact. The 'Eyes I dare not meet in dreams' are gone. The speaker dare not make eye contact for reasons unspecified: Because the eyes are accusatory? Because they are erotic? We do not know. We know only that they are metamorphosed, transfigured, disguised. More evasion: the eyes become 'Sunlight on a broken column'. Which, for the hollow men, is bad enough: 'Let me be no nearer.' The speaker is avoiding some difficult, but unspecified human problem. The image of the guy morphs into the image of the scarecrow: 'Let me also wear / Such deliberate disguises / Rat's coat, crowskin, crossed staves / In a field . . . '

(Unsurprisingly, given Eliot's lifelong poetic preoccupation with the failure to live, we have encountered this moral cowardice before, in 'Portrait of a Lady', where the lady's unlooked-for honesty has the callow young man suddenly discomfited and running for cover: 'And I must borrow every changing shape / To find expression . . . dance, dance / Like a dancing bear, / Cry like a parrot, chatter like an ape.')

In section III Eliot resumes the desert topos of *The Waste Land* and the basically unpunctuated mode of 'What the Thunder Said'. 'This is the dead land / This is cactus land'. He presents religion not as a sign of spirituality, but as evasion, as substitution, as transference: 'Trembling with tenderness / Lips that would kiss / Form prayers to broken stone.' Here, prayer is 'The supplication of a dead man's hand'—everyone in Limbo being dead, of course. The trembling lips are a reminiscence of Dante's Paolo and Francesca—'la bocca mi baciò tutto tremante' [kissed my mouth all trembling]— which Eliot quotes in his essay on Dante. The central point, though, is not the reminiscence, but the process of transference: physical desire is repackaged and re-presented to the self as a religious impulse. It is not only a disguise, but also a cop out and a travesty.

Section IV is more difficult to read cogently. The previous two sections have sketched the landscape of Limbo as presided over by 'a fading star'. Appropriately enough for 'a twilight kingdom', the star's flickering is interpreted as faltering rather than kindling. In section IV, Limbo is specifically 'this valley of dying stars'—an eternity of entropy. The eyes are absent still, but still feared—feared almost as Bill Sikes fears in *Oliver Twist* the eyes of the murdered Nancy.[10]

The section shows some 'development'—not only are the feared eyes absent, there are 'no eyes here' at all. Blindness has supervened, or there is nothing to be seen in the dying light: 'Sightless, unless . . .' Unless a transformation takes place and the feared eyes become 'the perpetual star / Multifoliate rose'—'perpetual' as opposed to the fading star of previous sections and the 'dying stars' of this one.

This 'visionary' possibility, however, is immediately dismissed. It is yet another transposition, another displacement of awkward human materials: it is 'The hope only / Of empty men.' After all, 'these paltry' are already rejected by heaven.

The final section, V, is a catalogue of failures to issue in action. (Remember: 'It is better, in a paradoxical way, to do evil than to do nothing.') The section begins with a parody of 'Here we go round the mulberry bush', which isn't simply a nursery rhyme, but describes behaviour that is enigmatically empty. Why do we go round the prickly pear? It is a perfect, quasi-ritualised pointless activity that symbolises the life fundamentally unlived.

Something—'the Shadow'—interrupts, intervenes between the impulse and the action. Even orgasm is suspended: 'Between the desire / And the spasm . . . Falls the Shadow.' Prayer, too, is blighted with aporia[11]: 'For Thine is'; 'For Thine is the'.

Finally, Eliot envisages the end of the world. 'Some say the world will end in fire', Robert Frost says in 'Fire and Ice', 'Some say in ice.' Eliot's alternatives are already resolved. It won't be a bang, but a whimper. It isn't absolutely clear that Eliot is speaking globally. Or whether he is restricting himself to the death of those in Limbo, 'these paltry, who never were alive'. There may be, too, a contrast between Guy Fawkes and the dummy, between the 'lost, violent' Boudin type, planning an explosion, and the hollow type.

It is possible to summarise the evasion of life in *The Hollow Men* in terms of eye contact—the absolute lack of it. The damned who have gone to Hell have 'direct eyes'. Those stuck in Limbo, in 'death's dream kingdom', are relieved to find that the eyes they fear have been transfigured, disguised as 'Sunlight on a broken column'. Religion and prayer are sublimations—erotic desire disguised. Section IV resumes the motif: 'There are no eyes here.' The eyes can be faced only when disguised—as 'the perpetual star / Multifoliate rose'. Section V, the final section, is a paean to procrastination, a stammer of inconclusiveness and inaction: 'For Thine is / Life is / For Thine is the.'

Ash-Wednesday (1930) is a great poem about renunciation, about the ascetic path to enlightenment—and its difficulties. As Eliot remarked in his Pascal essay (1931), 'the Christian thinker ... proceeds by rejection and elimination'. Eliot is actually revisiting the idea of the failure to live—but he is looking at it through the other end of the telescope, not as a failure, but as something possibly desirable. A conscious, positive decision to reject life differs from the *failure* to live.

In *The Mill on the Floss*, Philip Wakem is appalled by Maggie Tulliver's embrace of Christian asceticism. Maggie's reading of Thomas à Kempis creates in her 'a strange thrill of awe' because it requires not just virtue and fervent devotion but 'that having left all, he leave himself, and go wholly out of himself, and retain nothing of self-love'. Even cursory, baffled readers of *Ash-Wednesday* will recognise this hypnotic simplicity. We encounter it again when Eliot, in 'Francis Herbert Bradley', quotes Bradley's injunction from *Ethical Studies*: 'You must resolve to give up your will, as the mere will of this or that man, and you must put your whole self, your entire will, into the will of the divine.'

Simple enough: Dante's '*in la sua voluntade è nostra pace*' [Our peace in His will].

Simple enough in intention perhaps. *Ash-Wednesday*, though, is Eliot's most difficult poem, as Eliot himself ruefully and humorously conceded in his introduction to *The Use of Poetry and the Use of Criticism*: 'If a poem of mine entitled *Ash-Wednesday* ever goes into a second edition, I have thought of prefixing to it the lines of Byron from *Don Juan*': viz 'I don't pretend that I quite understand / My own meaning when I would be *very* fine. '

Walt Whitman's 'Shut Not Your Doors' (one of the 'Inscriptions' prefacing *Leaves of* Grass) claims 'The words of my book nothing, the drift of it every thing'. I have outlined the 'drift' of *Ash-Wednesday*. It is a poem about the difficulty of religious belief, about the difficulty of renouncing the temporal world. But the words, the detail of the poem are vital to our sometimes-strained comprehension of the whole. As Rosencrantz says in Tom Stoppard's *Rosencrantz and Guildenstern Are Dead*, words are 'what we depend on'. I will, therefore, elucidate the poem, section by section, beginning with the background. In the Christian calendar, Ash Wednesday, the sixth Wednesday before Easter, is the first day of Lent. Ashes are smudged on the foreheads of communicants to remind them of death, of sorrow for sins and the necessity for change and improvement.

Section I is a confession of despair, an avowal of renunciation, and a resignation, a submission to God's will. The poem begins with incomplete phrases, as incomplete phrases end *The Hollow Men*. Readers tend to miss the rhyme scheme in the general

fragmentedness—'turn' / 'mourn'; 'scope' / 'hope' and so on. The consistent ground note is lack of hope: 'Because I do not hope to turn again / Because I do not hope / Because I do not hope to turn . . . '

Eliot's source here is Guido Cavalcanti's 'Perch'io non spero di tornar giammai'—a poem of exile, of yearning for return, which Cavalcanti sent to his beloved in Tuscany to tell her of his sorrow and ill-health.

But the 'allusion' to Cavalcanti represents a recurrent mistake in readings of Eliot's poetry—the idea, dear to the academic mind, that recondite knowledge, the identification of a source, will unlock the meaning of a poem. After a lifetime during which learning was studiously applied to his poems like dusty, defunct electrodes, Eliot finally began to rebel in 'The Frontiers of Criticism' (1956). 'One can explain a poem by investigating what it is made of and the causes that brought it about; and explanation may be a necessary preparation for understanding. But to understand a poem it is also necessary . . . that we should endeavour to grasp what the poetry was aiming to be.'

Ash-Wednesday opens with the thrice-repeated cry of despair— 'Because I do not hope'—which is more important than Eliot's borrowing from Cavalcanti.[12]

Of course, the cry 'Because I do not hope' is twice inflected— 'to turn again'; 'to turn'. Turn where? What are the bases of this despair? 'Turn again' means 'turn back' to what is past. In the first stanza of section I, ambition, youth, and accomplishments are all seen as aspects of the past, irrevocably behind the speaker who can only be Eliot, the advocate of impersonality, in this his most personal poem.

In 'Because I do not hope [i.e. it is impossible] to turn', 'to turn' has two different senses: of not knowing which way to turn, and of being unable to turn back. So Eliot is unable to return to the past, can see no clear future, and is therefore in despair: 'Because I do not hope.' This is roughly the position described by Hopkins in stanza 3 of 'The Wreck of the Deutschland': Hopkins's own conversion begins with two negatives, the fear of God in him and the dread of Hell, which is resolved in a flight of faith to God. Similarly, Eliot's despair compels him to God: 'Consequently I rejoice, having to construct something / Upon which to rejoice.' In his essay on F. H. Bradley (1927), he articulated the related notion that 'scepticism and disillusion are a useful equipment for religious understanding'.

Though this central thrust of Eliot's argument is easy to follow, there are local difficulties. The second stanza of section I laments the loss of 'The infirm glory of the positive hour', which is also 'The one veritable transitory power'. *Infirm. Transitory.* Yet, a power that transports Eliot to an idealised place where 'springs flow' and 'trees *flower* [my italics]'—as they do in Perugino's backgrounds—rather than 'bloom' or 'blossom'. What is this uncertain, intermittent power? We are not told precisely, so we have to guess what this transfiguring power is that can make trees *flower*. It could be poetry. Or it could be love. But if it is poetry it is followed by loss of inspiration. If love, followed by the failure of love. It is 'an *infirm* glory', a '*transitory* power'.

But I think it is happiness, pure and simple. And that happiness has gone for good.

The landscape is not actual but symbolic of a mental state. The present is arid: 'I cannot drink'; 'for there is nothing again'. We infer from what is lost—flowering trees, spring waters—that the speaker is in a desert place, sunk in unhappiness, in despair.

In stanza 3 of section I, Eliot renounces 'the blessèd face'. Who is female, nameless, and unidentified at this point in the poem— in fact, never fully elucidated. She is not the Virgin Mary—as we discover irrefutably (to jump ahead) in section II, where 'this Lady', we learn, 'honours the Virgin in meditation'. If she honours the Virgin, she cannot *be* the Virgin. She is, it transpires (to jump ahead again) in section IV, a nameless woman 'in Mary's colour'— who is both ordinary and charismatic, one who can impart grace to existence, one who straddles the world of the spirit and the mundane world quite unconsciously: 'Talking of trivial things / In ignorance and in knowledge of eternal dolour.' This is the person whose 'blessèd face' Eliot renounces in section I, along with his past ambitions and achievements, and the possibility of happiness.

This triple renunciation, 'for there is nothing again', functions like Descartes's wholesale doubt in *Meditations on First Philosophy* and the *Discourse on Method*—in which doubt is not piecemeal, instance by instance, but absolute. The method is to doubt everything—and see what, if anything, resists doubt. In this way, you reach bedrock, the very bottom, and build on that. It is related to Eliot's exposition of the *via negativa*[13] in *East Coker*: 'what you do not know is the only thing you know.'

Section II has an Old Testament desert scenario. It rejoices in the annihilation and dispersal of the body—achieved thanks to the intercession of a woman in white, a Lady who prays to the Virgin. It celebrates, too, the loss of ego in larger spiritual purpose: 'As I am forgotten / And would be forgotten, so I would forget / Thus devoted, concentrated in purpose.' Section II embraces extinction. It opens with the three immaculate and notorious leopards. Asked what the lines meant, Eliot merely repeated them. The leopards are spiritual because spotless, immaculate. As readers we have to accept the downright biblical desert scenario as Eliot presents it to us. Or perhaps Dante is a better analogue than the Bible for Eliot's imaginative procedures here—those swift, authoritative impositions, those unquestionable 'realities'. The 'reality' here is 'The Garden / Where all love ends'—a site of renunciation that is 'the quiet of the desert' and the shade of a juniper tree. That *juniper* tree provides more than shade. To the reader, it provides conviction. It is a reality effect. *Juniper*—inessential, optional even, rhythmically interchangeable with 'sycamore'. Without it, the self would still be consumed by the spiritual leopards but the scene would carry less irrefutable conviction for the reader.

The bones rejoice in the renunciation of the self: body, desire, and deeds are consigned thankfully to oblivion. The bones are grateful, they shine 'because of the goodness of this Lady', who seems to be a catalyst in the process, without being directly responsible. The bones that remain address the Lady in a series of paradoxes. Why? These paradoxes—'Calm and distressed', 'Worried reposeful'—underscore the Lady's impossible status, her hybrid nature, somewhere between the mystical and the mundane, 'Talking of trivial things / In ignorance and in knowledge of eternal dolour', as section IV has it.

Section III describes the speaker's upward progress on three spiral staircases, with a mimetic ongoing coil of rhymes—'stair' five times, 'banister', 'air', 'wears', 'despair' twice, 'repair', 'hair'. The stairs are a metaphor for spiritual ascent—an ascent hampered by hope, by despair, and by a vision of sensuous loveliness. The stairs themselves have no descriptive fixity: the first stair, with a banister, is obscured by 'the vapour in the fetid air'; the second stair is dark, damp, decayed; the third is medieval with a 'slotted window bellied like the fig's fruit'. We infer that the ascent is essentially spiritual—partly because, below him, Eliot can see himself (the 'same shape') struggling still with 'the devil of the stairs'.[14] Spiritual, then, because physically impossible.

As he ascends, Eliot leaves behind the three temptations—he renounces hope, despair, and physical love associated with Pan. Since *Ash-Wednesday* begins with despair and proceeds to rejoicing, 'having to construct something / Upon which to rejoice', it follows logically that despair and hope are 'deceitful'—or crudely opposed categories at the very least, a bit like those 'two impostors' in Kipling's 'If', 'Triumph' and 'Disaster'.

Pan is more complicated than hope and despair: 'The broadbacked figure drest in blue and green / Enchanted the maytime with an antique flute.' For a start, he is not named as Pan by Eliot. He is merely the 'broadbacked figure' playing the flute. The flute, however, is a familiar prop. The magic flute played by Papageno in Mozart's opera is a set of panpipes. And in this case the flute is appropriately 'antique', an archaic quality insisted on, too, in Eliot's use of 'drest' rather than 'dressed'. This Pan figure is serenading a magnetic amorous epitome: 'Blown hair is sweet, brown hair over the mouth blown, / Lilac and brown hair.' This evocation has all the tactile potency of 'La Figlia Che Piange': 'Her hair over her arms and her arms full of flowers.' And this delicately erotic topos—characterised by flesh visible through hair—is rejected as 'distraction' by the climber of the stairs.

Section IV is an account of involuntary or quasi-involuntary intercession by the Lady—the same Lady of sections I and II, 'the silent sister' 'in Mary's colour'. She intimates salvation from death—whispers of immortality from the yew tree! And she produces blessèd conditions—'made strong the fountains and made fresh the springs'—without design.

Is it possible to characterise her more fully? She is another of Eliot's hybrids—like the 'familiar compound ghost' of *Little Gidding*, 'Both intimate and unidentifiable'; like *The Waste Land*'s Stetson, inhabitant of twentieth-century London and sailor at Mylae in 260 BC. She is a temporal woman with an eternal dimension: 'White light folded, sheathed about her, folded.'

Is she a nun? After all, she is 'veiled in white and blue' and in the next section she is 'the veiled sister', which could be a reference to taking the veil. She would, then, be a woman who has renounced the world and its works—in this poem about renunciation. Has she taken a vow of silence? She says nothing, yet speaks through the 'thousand whispers from the yew'. She also exercises extraordinary powers. A sign from her brings temperateness—fountains, springs, birdsong—to a desert environment: 'Made cool the dry rock and made firm the sand.'

In summary, because the nun 'moves in the time between sleep and waking', she is able to redeem the time, to redeem the dream— 'the unread vision in the higher dream'. Which is what exactly? What does it mean to redeem the time? I will try to explain.

Section IV begins with a grammatical ambiguity: 'Who walked between the violet and the violet' is not punctuated with the expected question mark. It is therefore stranded between a question and a statement; a statement whose subject is occluded and whose expected second half is also occluded. (As it might be, for example, [The cat] who sat on the mat [is a marmalade cat].) This grammatical ambiguity, which is extended all through section IV, mirrors and expresses a temporal ambiguity that is crucial. On the one hand, there is familiar, standard Greenwich Mean Time. On the other hand, we are allowed to glimpse a more fugitive time: 'The new years', 'the years that walk between'. The new years and the nun are elided. As the nun 'walked', so the new years 'walk'. This is the redeemed time, time that has been retrieved, renewed, changed. It is, therefore, time in which miracles can take place, in which the inviolable temporal chain can be broken. The nun is at once in normal time *and* 'in the time between sleep and waking'. In normal time, we die. In redeemed time, 'between sleep and waking', we do not die: 'the wind shake[s] a thousand whispers from the yew [traditionally associated with death].'

The redemption of time is opposed to the image of the unicorns: 'While jewelled unicorns draw by the gilded hearse.' Precious stones and metals—'jewelled', 'gilded'—are staple props of the eternal in Old and Middle English visionary poems such as 'The Dream of the Rood' or *Pearl*. But here, I think, Eliot intends an image of perpetual death: an incorruptible hearse drawn by extinct mythic beasts. It is *this* perpetual death that is overthrown when 'a thousand whispers' are shaken from the yew tree traditionally associated with death.[15] Where before there was a deathly silence, there are now 'whispers'. The redemption of time is, therefore, the promise of life after death, a promise implicit in the yew's evergreenness.

Section V describes those who are unable to surrender themselves to God, no matter how firmly they set their minds. The opening, though, isn't easy to summarise. It has two arguments. The first is that even when language fails, the Word survives. The Word, of course, is God.

The second argument is about belief in God. *Ash-Wednesday* is often read as a poem arising out of Eliot's religious conversion— as a poem of belief; it is in fact a poem about the visceral nature of faith, the difficulty of true belief. We talk about things having a mind of their own. Eliot's refinement is to observe that the mind has a mind of its own. Faith cannot be willed or argued into exist- ence. When, in 1936, Eliot describes *In Memoriam* as a great poem of religious doubt, not faith, he is, I think, also reorienting misreadings of *Ash-Wednesday*. In 'The "Pensées" of Pascal' (1931), he maintains that 'the demon of doubt . . . is inseparable from the spirit of belief'.

In 1930, Eliot had been a member of the Anglo-Catholic communion for three years. His attitude to religion was pub- licly uncompromising: he didn't want religion to make any ac- commodation with the secular impulse. In 'Religion and Literature' (1935), he is certain that modern literature is 'simply unaware of, simply cannot understand the meaning of, the pri- macy of the supernatural over the natural life'. *Ash-Wednesday* ar- gues precisely this position—the primacy of the supernatural over the natural life—*and fails.* It is possible to argue that, therefore, the poetry is truer to reality than Eliot's theoretical position. But the difficulty of true religion was precisely what attracted Eliot. Its re- quirements are intractable, absolute—and difficult to fulfil. Were they not difficult, they would not be worth struggling towards.

In 'Thoughts after Lambeth' (1931) Eliot argues that 'Youth' will be more attracted by 'a difficult religion than to an easy one', a religion that has not been 'robbed of the severity of its demands'. This toughness is echoed in a footnote to 'Baudelaire in Our Time' (1929), in which Eliot extols this maxim: 'the spirit killeth, but the letter giveth life'. Eliot sets the bar high, deliberately, consciously—aware, therefore, that he and we might not clear it.

The speaker asks the 'veiled sister' to pray for those 'who chose thee and oppose thee'. These are not simply believers who are sinners. They are those who live in existential contradiction—what is known as *mauvaise foi,* bad faith. Then there are those 'who affirm before the world and deny between the rocks'. Again, this isn't hypocrisy of the kind recommended by the Spirit (Mephistopheles) to Clough's Dipsychus: 'You'll go to church of course, you know; / Or at the least will take a pew / To send your wife and servants to. / Trust me, I make a point of that; / No infidelity, that's flat.' 'Denying between the rocks' is, rather, a fundamental fissure in the self that thinks it *does* believe but ultimately, privately, does not. And there are those who are drawn to belief but cannot make even the first step: 'Who will not go away and cannot pray.' And there are those who are 'terrified'—either of God, or a Godless existence—and whose terror makes it impossible for them to surrender themselves to the obvious good. They are petrified in the moment and rescue is impossible.

So, to summarise: God, the Word, exists; but for a variety of reasons people find it difficult to accept the Word, difficult to believe in God. Or, to alter the emphasis fractionally, although, in their very different ways, these unbelievers cannot hear the Word, it nevertheless exists.

There is a plethora of internal rhyming in section V, some of it so contrived as to verge on the inept: 'the mainland' and 'the rain land' just taking the withered laurels from 'silence' and 'islands' or 'rejoice', 'noise', and 'voice'. We are all of us familiar with the poem whose real subject is less important than its rhyme scheme.

F. T. Prince's 'Soldiers Bathing', for instance. Reading such a poem is like watching show jumping at Hickstead. At intervals, there are obstacles to be surmounted, rhymes to be achieved. Once surmounted, the next obstacle looms large. What takes place between these obstacles is purely secondary—a matter of momentum. At this point in *Ash-Wednesday*, many of Eliot's readers, already under interpretative strain, must have fallen—distracted by the sympathetic automatism of their lifting legs. As Auden had it, '"O where are you going?" said reader to rider.'

There is an answer to that question. Alas. Eliot's second loquacious, rhyme-led paragraph 'argues' that our failure to hear the Word is because the noise of the temporal drowns out the spiritual. Compared to Eliot's differentiated micronotations of belief, this is so conventional a thought, so theologically trite, that one is scarcely surprised by the distracting 'noise' of the rhymes.

The last two lines of section V are less enigmatic than they might initially seem: 'The desert in the garden the garden in the desert / Of drouth, spitting from the mouth the withered apple-seed.' Man's fall, invoked in 'the withered apple-seed', had linguistic consequences, namely the confusion of languages, according to some theologians. Eliot seems to have been of this persuasion. In *After Strange Gods* (1933), he speaks of original sin as 'a very real and tremendous thing'. There, Eliot's version of fallen language is Arnoldian in configuration, with its lack of a central authority and the plethora of competing individual voices. So, 'spitting from the mouth the withered apple-seed' is a manner of speaking—of speaking a fallen, corrupted language. 'The desert in the garden the garden in the desert' isn't simply a trite mystical chiasmus, however. It is a way of saying that, just as the Fall was present in Eden, so salvation is possible in the most exhausted ground.

In the next section, VI, we are about to meet another intractable temperament unable to give itself to the love of God to the exclusion of all else—Eliot, the poet helplessly infatuated, hopelessly in love with our beautiful world, and unable to renounce its gorgeous illusion.

Section VI repeats and alters the opening phrases of the poem: not '*Because* I do not hope', but '*Although* I do not hope'. At the beginning of *Ash-Wednesday*, Eliot floated the following proposition: *because* he is in a condition of despair, he will seek salvation in renunciation. The changed word '*although*' prepares us for the contrary. (Compare: 'Because I am ninety years old, I think I will die soon' versus 'Although I am ninety years old, I do not think I will die for a long time.') At the end of his poem, *although* he is equally without hope, he turns again; he is unable to renounce the temporal world—although he knows the temporal world to be an illusion. Life, the time 'between birth and dying', is a 'brief transit' made up of dreams: 'this brief transit where dreams cross / The dreamcrossed twilight between birth and dying.' And the dreams are false. They come through the ivory gates, not the gates of horn: 'the blind eye creates / The empty forms between the ivory gates.'

Like the backsliders and recidivists in the previous section, Eliot would like to do otherwise: 'I do not wish to wish these things.' However, 'The weak spirit quickens to rebel.'

He wishes for the earth, which he cannot renounce as the illusion he knows it to be—a distraction from the claims of eternity. Nine lines or so of the most beautiful poetry in English bring the world indelibly before us. They are drenched in desire, rapt with repetition, in love with every charged particular. It is Eliot's indestructible *Das Lied von der Erde*. Look at his repeated use of the word 'lost' and you see the lines are also his 'temps perdu', a memory of happiness:

> From the wide window towards the granite shore
> The white sails still fly seaward, seaward flying
> Unbroken wings
>
> And the lost heart stiffens and rejoices
> In the lost lilac and the lost sea voices
> And the weak spirit quickens to rebel
> For the bent golden-rod and the lost sea smell
> Quickens to recover
> The cry of the quail and the whirling plover

This memory of happiness, Eliot also knows, is 'the *infirm* glory of the positive hour'—a thing that, at the beginning of the poem, he had not thought to experience again. He therefore concludes with a prayer to the Virgin and to the 'blessèd sister'. And he prays for resignation, obedience—and freedom from the falsehood he has just so stunningly hymned into being.[16]

In 'Thoughts after Lambeth' (1931) Eliot records that his conversion is regarded by the *Times Literary Supplement* as an eccentric anachronism, a desertion from the standard of progress. Even allowing for exaggeration, it is clear that Eliot really believes that the new orthodoxy is humanist and sceptical. Religion is a threatened minority interest. Looking back, we see Moral Re-armament—in which Eliot's religious pageant play *The Rock* played a significant part—as evidence of religious resurgence. Then, it seemed a necessary crusade, a militancy required by a threatened religion. How, then, does one write religious poetry in 1930? Should one choose the hallowed, traditional register, or the contemporary demotic?

A metaphor: Eliot goes for the traditional single malt, with what whisky tasters call 'notes' of the subtly contemporary. The end of section I, for example, returns to the imagery of the beginning, 'Why should the agèd eagle stretch its wings?' Its penultimate stanza begins: 'Because these wings are no longer wings to fly / But merely vans to beat the air / The air which is now thoroughly small and dry . . . ' The passage in its entirety is rhetorically interesting, because its registers are so mixed—the archaic is tinged with the conversational and everyday. On the one hand, the wings become 'vans', a shift that goes with the earlier accents on 'agèd' and 'blessèd'. On the other hand, there is the thoroughly prosaic and modern colloquial note sounded by the intensifier 'thoroughly'. In a lexis tinged with prayer, 'thoroughly' strikes the ear as *forcibly ordinary*, akin to the intensifier in John Betjeman's 'In a Bath Teashop': 'She, such a very ordinary little woman.' *Very*.

Equally interesting is the poetry of abstract statement, the renunciation of the concrete and the figurative, in the imperatives 'Teach us to care and not to care / Teach us to sit still'. Important for Eliot here is the general example of Pound's repetition and variation in *Hugh Selwyn Mauberley*: 'some from fear of weakness / some from fear of censure . . . '[17]

The high point of this abstract technique is in section II: 'Terminate torment / Of love unsatisfied / The greater torment / Of love satisfied.' The thought here is similar to the paradox of Wilde's *Lady Windemere's Fan*: 'In this world there are only two tragedies. One is not getting what one wants, and the other is getting it. The last is much the worst; the last is a real tragedy.' But what is cynicism in Wilde is dark wisdom in Eliot, expressed with exact rhetorical balance. We readers may have the illusion that we are responding to the naked sentiment—what Wallace Stevens called the poetry of philosophy—but we are also responding to Eliot's artful arrangement of rhyming sentiment. As with all rhyme, there is repetition and change, identity and difference.

Ash-Wednesday was published in April 1930. In September, Eliot published 'Marina', another poem of renunciation:

> Those who sharpen the tooth of the dog, meaning
> Death
> Those who glitter with the glory of the hummingbird, meaning
> Death
> Those who sit in the sty of contentment, meaning
> Death
> Those who suffer the ecstasy of the animals, meaning
> Death
>
> Are become insubstantial

On the whole, readers find this the least appealing section of 'Marina'. But it is important to understand exactly *what* is falling away from Pericles, what is 'become insubstantial'—otherwise, modern readers are likely to react adversely to what they identify incorrectly as sexual distaste in the phrase 'suffer the ecstasy of animals'. In point of fact, Eliot is setting out four of the seven deadly sins.[18] In order, they are: gluttony ('the tooth of the dog'); pride ('the glory of the hummingbird'); sloth ('the sty of contentment'); and lust. Typically, Eliot takes the familiar, the clichéd, the threadbare, and restores its power. Compare 'the infirm glory of the positive hour', Eliot's profound periphrasis for the invisible familiar, 'happiness'. And how intelligent to have only four of the seven sins—as a prophylactic against facile shortcuts to the worn originals. Without the conventional word 'sin' or the quantity 'seven' to assist us, we are detained, puzzled, re-educated. What a difference, too, it makes to replace 'deadly' with 'meaning / Death'—itself a version of Romans 6:23, 'the wages of sin is death'.

Like the other Ariel poems, 'Marina' charts the shared border between the old and the new, exploring the shared tissue joining the end of one thing with the beginning of something else. The poem is spoken by Pericles to his daughter Marina. Pericles hasn't seen Marina since birth and believes she has been murdered. In Shakespeare's play, Pericles (and we the audience) are particularly moved that Marina should so exactly replicate her mother, Thaisa. Thaisa's 'death' in childbirth is an end that is also a beginning: 'Thaisa was my mother, who did end / The minute I began.'[19]

In 'Portrait of a Lady', Eliot ironically apportions to the lady the cliché of death as the end of life's journey. She refers to herself as 'one about to reach her journey's end'. Compare the equally fatigued figure in the 'Hades' episode of *Ulysses*: the tramp 'emptying the dirt and stones out of his huge dustbrown yawning boot. After life's journey.' In 'Marina', Eliot reconceives the cliché, presents it obliquely, allusively, literalises the metaphor. Essentially, Pericles is portrayed at the end of his journey, approaching his unknown destination—'what seas what shores what granite islands'. The decay of his body is transposed to his vessel: 'The garboard strake leaks, the seams need caulking.' What he is going towards is what he has left behind—'What images *return*'—a lost childhood memory:

> I made this, I have forgotten
> And remember.

Clearly, Eliot is giving us a subtly intelligent version of the second childhood.[20] That old deathbed familiar has been given a re-fit: 'Whispers and small laughter between leaves and hurrying feet'.

This is a topos Eliot will revisit in *Burnt Norton*, where it is again associated with children: 'for the leaves were full of children, / Hidden excitedly, containing laughter.'

Chronologically, Pericles is journeying to an end which was his beginning. Spatially, towards 'granite islands', and also towards a face. 'This face' is the face of his daughter—which *in extremis* comes and goes, 'less clear and clearer'. When I say *in extremis*, I mean death itself. Hence the faltering, fluctuating pulse in the arm, 'less strong and stronger'.

Dutch painters of still life were almost required to demonstrate their virtuosity by rendering the mother-of-pearl of an oyster shell and, more testingly, it was thought, a coil of lemon peel. Hockney's *A Bigger Splash* confronts the challenge of fixing in paint the momentary and unstoppably fluid. In *Black Dogs*, Ian McEwan manages to describe something even more difficult—the absence of light. He makes darkness visible. In 'Marina', Eliot joins the select body of writers who have attempted to describe dying—and he succeeds without ever once alluding to his virtuosity. It is a quiet feat of genius.

Wittgenstein said that death was not an event in life—and therefore beyond our mental competence to speculate about. But dying *is* an event in life, and Chekhov brings it to book in 'Ward No. 6', taking us into the head of the dying Dr. Ragin: 'a herd of deer, extraordinarily beautiful and graceful, which he had been reading about on the previous day, raced past him; then a peasant woman stretched out a hand to him with a registered letter . . . The postmaster said something. Then everything vanished, and Dr. Ragin lost consciousness for ever.'

Artificially grouped together, the list of such attempts looks longer than it is. D. H. Lawrence's 'The Prussian Officer', Elizabeth Bishop's last 'Sonnet', Emily Dickinson's 'I heard a Fly buzz when I died', Hemingway's 'The Snows of Kilimanjaro', Kundera's *Life Is Elsewhere*, Golding's *The Spire*, Bergotte's death in *A la recherche du temps perdu*, Nabokov's 'Perfection', Betjeman's 'Cottage Hospital', Browning's 'Prospice', *Anna Karenina*, *Madame Bovary*, and Hemingway's epigraph to 'Big Two-Hearted River' are all attempts to describe this indescribable moment. In Tolstoy's 'The Death of Ivan Ilyich', a few hours before Ilyich dies, we are told, in a remarkable passage, that he feels like someone being forced into a sack and then that he experiences a confused sensation—like being on a train and thinking it's going in a different direction, before realising the truth.[21]

This is Hemingway making us privy to the death of a bullfighter: 'Maera felt everything getting larger and larger and then smaller and smaller. Then it got larger and larger and then smaller and smaller. Then everything commenced to run faster and faster as when they speed up a cinematograph film. Then he was dead.'

The best of these crypto-séances into the dying consciousness are the Dickinson, the Chekhov—and the Eliot, which is brilliantly vicarious and exploits poetry's relaxed attitude to the formalities of syntax and punctuation to create something more suggestive, more semantically porous than prose. Compare the tough simplicity of Hemingway's repetition with Eliot's 'What seas what shores what grey rocks' and you see at once a certain primitivism in Hemingway. Eliot has only to omit the question mark and his questions double as exclamations. Or consider 'the woodthrush singing through fog'. Which becomes, weirdly, 'the woodsong fog' before reverting to 'woodthrush calling through the fog'. What a difference there is between a woodthrush 'singing' and a woodthrush 'calling'. 'Calling' carries a connotation, vestigial perhaps, of calling to a particular object. As if the thrush had a message for Pericles, as if he were being called home.

I said that Pericles was journeying towards a face. The face belongs to Marina, and thence to offspring, to children, to progeny: 'this life / Living to live in a world of time beyond me.' His old vessel is frail, dilapidated but he rejoices in 'the *new* ships'. I can do no better here than quote Robert Lowell's (more explicit but still moving) framing of the same sentiment in his poem 'Obit':

> I'm for and with myself in my otherness,
>
> in the eternal return of earth's fairer children
>
> the lily, the rose, the sun on rose and brick,
>
> the loved, the lover, and their fear of life,
>
> their unconquered flux, insensate oneness, their painful
>
>   'it was . . . '

The romantic Eliot regretted the buried feelings left unfulfilled and rued the cautious circumspection of our sluggish hearts. The ascetic Eliot, though, could see the virtue of renunciation—and its difficulty. He writes, therefore, about the failure of feeling in poems like 'Gerontion', 'Animula', and *The Hollow Men*. At the same time, in *Ash-Wednesday*, he shows us the worthy obverse of this position—the ascetic renunciation which *chooses* to turn its back on pleasure, on the temporal, on sensuous emotion, on the self itself, the better to embrace eternal verities. And finds that his will to renounce the temporary illusion of the temporal is weaker than his helpless passion for the natural world.

Elsewhere in his oeuvre, the alert classicist Eliot was determined to cross-examine every careless claim to passion, as the next chapter will show.

Two

ELIOT AS CLASSICIST:
THE ENQUIRY INTO
FEELINGS

ELIOT WASN'T ONLY THE POSSUM. He was also, briefly, a kiwi. In a letter to his cousin, Eleanor Hinkley (26 April 1911), Eliot describes a visit to the London Zoo, where he 'gave the apterix a bun'. Seven years later, T. S. Apteryx, the correct spelling, was Eliot's chosen pseudonym for two reviews he wrote for *The Egoist*—the first of *Poetry 1916–17* edited by Edward Marsh (March 1918) and the second of Gilbert Cannan and Alice Meynell (April 1918). In C. K. Stead's novel *Mansfield*, Stead has Eliot explain to Katherine Mansfield that he has chosen the national symbol of her country, New Zealand, because it is a flightless bird—and therefore anti-romantic. The explanation is a guess, of course, but a shrewd one.

Eliot the anti-romantic had a gift for subtle and not so subtle comic bathos. It is a frequent technique in the early poetry and an instinctive disposition. This is Eliot, in *The Use of Poetry*, slyly letting the air out of Pater's famous formulation that all art aspires to the condition of music: 'From one point of view, the poet aspires to the condition of the music-hall comedian.' (He is writing about popularity.)

Anti-romantic. Writing of Dante's *Vita Nuova*, Eliot defines the word's penumbra:

> there is also a practical sense of realities behind it, which is anti-romantic: not to expect more from *life* than it can give or more from *human* beings than they can give; to look to *death* for what life cannot give. The *Vita Nuova* belongs to 'vision literature'; but its philosophy is the Catholic philosophy of disillusion.

Disillusion.

We need look no farther than 'Lune De Miel', Eliot's disenchanted honeymoon narrative in *Poems 1920*. His honeymooners are thoroughly divested of any romantic impulses or characteristics. The poem is written in French and it's possible to detect the presence of four French writers in Eliot's text—Laforgue, Apollinaire, Maupassant, and Flaubert.

Laforgue is present in the description of the Byzantine basilica of Sant' Apollinare as 'Vieille usine désaffectée de Dieu' [a disused God factory]. Compare Laforgue's description of 'La Nature', in 'Complainte à Notre-Dame des Soirs', as an exhausted sap factory: 'fade / Usine de sève.' Both poets, then, use the idea of the factory as a synecdoche for the functional, for the anti-romantic—as a benchmark for (what else?) the workbench.

But overall, Eliot's tart, pitiless, unforgiving irony has none of Laforgue's wry, sprightly self-inculpation. Eliot's lovers are American. They hail from Terre Haute in Indiana, a location which allows Eliot a sly joke involving Pays Bas, the Low Countries. They lie between the sheets, sweating in the Ravenna heat, scratching at limbs swollen with bug bites. There is 'une forte odeur de chienne'—not generic, therefore, but a smell associated with the bitch—what Leopold Bloom (in 'Nausicaa') memorably calls 'a hogo you could hang your hat on'. The man's thoughts are a long way from spooning—let alone, in Nabokov's inimitable coinage, 'forking'. He thinks, rather, about tipping and writing up his accounts. I believe Eliot's poem at this point owes something to the initially inept honeymoon in Maupassant's *Une Vie*—where the sexually disgusted Jeanne is pained by her husband's inadequate tips. At any rate, Eliot's poem is resolute in its disgust and punitive contempt. It is knowingly, unapologetically unpleasant—an adjective we shall return to.

Sant' Apollinare was an ascetic. So we might expect him to function as an implicd contrast to the passionate honeymooners. Yet he proves to be more of an analogue. Except for an orgy of scratching, they appear to embrace asceticism rather than each other. The basilica and the couple are equally keeping up appearances: they are miserable, the sixth-century basilica is crumbling and disused, although it retains 'la forme précise de Byzance'. By invoking Saint Apollinare, you wonder if Eliot isn't also insinuating the ironic presence of Guillaume Apollinaire, author of the pornographic poem 'Les Onze Mille Verges' [the eleven thousand penises / rods].

The basic ironic mechanism of 'Lune De Miel' is to conflate the (non)sex with the itinerary through Europe. The ironic collocation of sex and place names was invented by Flaubert in *Madame Bovary*, when Léon takes Emma, sexually, for the first time, in a fiacre, whose route, street name after street name, an A to Z of Rouen, is given in deflating detail for over a page. It was the passage that Flaubert's friend and publisher, DuCamp, wished most fervently to drop. Flaubert resisted all other editorial changes—designed, the editors said, to free the narrative from allegedly 'superfluous' detail—but he conceded the cab episode. It was deleted and never appeared in the *Revue de Paris* where the novel was serialised. Passion might pass. But ridicule and prurience were out of the question. A caress was possible. Sex as an itch was 'impossible'. Eliot's poem, too, is replete with itching as he plays ironically with the etymology of 'prurience' ('dallying with lascivious thoughts': Latin *prurire*, to itch). We get the itch without the lasciviousness, just as the basilica retains its Byzantine form without any spiritual substance.

There is comparably determined anti-romantic subversion at the end of Eliot's third restaurant poem, 'Sweeney Among the Nightingales'. (The other two are 'Dans Le Restaurant' and 'Hysteria'.)

Eliot introduces his principals—there is the animalistic Sweeney, the lady in the Spanish cape, 'the silent man in mocha brown', and 'Rachel *née* Rabinovitch'. Those who believe Eliot is anti-Semitic think he is drawing attention to a surreptitious change in name. I'm not sure why this is thought to be anti-Semitic—unless changing your name is itself shameful because anti-Semitic and self-hating. (The choreographer Jerome Robbins was born Jerome Wilson Rabinowitz. Perhaps he just wanted, honourably enough, to assimilate.) Obviously, that maiden name, Rabinovitch, is Jewish, but it tells us, more importantly, that she is a married woman—importantly in a poem which is about adultery. Darkly about adultery because Eliot describes the actions of his principals minutely—without, however, offering us a cogent explanation. We have only the barest outlines of the enigmatic situation. If it is a dream—a thought suggested by the line 'And Sweeney guards the hornèd gate'—then it is a true one. Nevertheless, the oneiric status of the action will account for slippage in the narrative.

The circumstances are somewhat louche. One woman 'draws a stocking up'. Propositions, negotiations are in the air, but 'the man with heavy eyes / Declines the gambit'. Are we in a brothel? It would have to be top of the range. Instead of a bartender, there is a waiter with a walk-on part—which, I think, argues against the idea of a dive. So do the 'hot-house grapes', which sound rather expensive, because out of season. I think Eliot is telling us animal appetites flourish even in the most elevated social contexts—a Greek palace, or a private dining room.

In the penultimate stanza, 'Someone indistinct' arrives, whom we are encouraged to identify with Agamemnon returning from the Trojan wars to discover the adultery between his Queen Clytemnestra and Aegisthus—a situation that results in his murder. We deduce, therefore, that the 'Someone indistinct' is a wronged husband.

Eliot's anti-romantic emblem of these occluded circumstances is, paradoxically, the idea of the traditionally romantic nightingale. Nightingales are in pronounced contrast to the next-door nunnery, though I do not think it convincing to invoke the slang meaning of nightingale for prostitute, a meaning so rare it is unrecorded in the *OED*. 'The nightingales are singing near / the Convent of the Sacred Heart, // And sang within the bloody wood / When Agamemnon cried aloud / And let their liquid siftings fall . . . ' With this penultimate line, 'And let their liquid siftings fall', we are still in the romantic frame.

The poetically conventional adjective for the nightingale's song is 'liquid'. Compare Tennyson's 'Geraint and Enid' (from *The*

Idylls of the King). Geraint rides into the ruined castle court and first hears the voice of Enid singing.

> And [it] made him like a man abroad at morn
> When first the *liquid* [my italics] notes beloved of men
> Comes flying over many a windy wave
> To Britain, and in April suddenly
> Breaks from a coppice gemm'd with green and red,
> And he suspends his converse with a friend...
> To think or say, "There is the nightingale" . . .

It is only with Eliot's final line that we realise that 'liquid siftings' refers not to the song of the nightingale, but to its shit—beautifully, accurately, perfectly described: 'And let their liquid siftings fall / To stain the stiff dishonoured shroud.'[1]

The nightingale's song, the honeymoon . . . In Eliot's early poetry is nothing sacred? Very little. Not even the love song, which, in 'The Love Song of J. Alfred Prufrock', has attached to it a name of surpassing prosiness. Like Pope, the author of *Peri Bathous*, Eliot is a master of the art of sinking, of bathos.

In 1928, Eliot famously defined himself in his preface to *For Lancelot Andrewes*, as 'a classicist in literature, a royalist in politics, and anglo-catholic in religion'.[2]

What did Eliot mean by 'classicist in literature' in 1928, and before, when the great early poetry was being written? He means by classicist, I shall argue, a consciously anti-romantic stance—sceptical of theatrical, exaggerated emotion. This position has its roots in the late eighteenth century, when the advent of the novel of sensibility almost simultaneously summoned up its satirical antitype—Sterne's ironically emotional narrative of sexual tourism *A Sentimental Journey*, Jane Austen's *Sense and Sensibility*.

Eliot's position derives from three French thinkers—Julien Benda, Charles Maurras, and Pierre Lasserre—all of whom mistrusted emotion and saw an antidote in Reason.

But Eliot's declaration for the classicist position came in 1928. How informed was Eliot about classicism when he wrote the early poetry?

We know that he did not read Julien Benda, a key classicist thinker, until 13 July 1920—when he writes to Pound on a post-card, '*Belphégor* received and much pleased with it. If you can procure any other of J.B.'s works I will purchase them from you.'[3] On 10 August 1920, Eliot writes to Scofield Thayer, editor of *The Dial*, about *Belphégor*: 'Benda's book is ripping. I hope you can print it in full.'

Yet by October 1920, only two-three months after first reading Benda, behold! in a letter to the *TLS*, Eliot is confidently invoking Benda and agreeing when Benda stigmatises his fellow classicist Maurras as a 'romantic'. Benda—wilfully clever, a little perversely—convicts Maurras of being excessively emotional in his advocacy of anti-emotional classicist principles. Benda calls it 'the Romanticism of Reason'.[4]

And the gist of Eliot's *TLS* letter is interesting because it appears to dispense with the crucial opposition of classicist and romantic. So, here is Eliot, on 28 October 1920, writing to the *Times Literary Supplement* that 'it would perhaps be beneficial if we employed both terms ['romanticism' and 'classicism'] as little as possible, if we even forgot these terms altogether'. Yet, only eight years later, in 1928, he was defining himself as a classicist.

This letter to the *TLS* doesn't sound like a tyro ticking off his superiors. It sounds like someone who is confident, informed, and expert. It isn't a good letter, however. It is pernickety without clarity. For our purpose, there is one moment of useful lucidity. Eliot notes that Cyril Falls, a contributor to the *TLS* correspondence, volunteers that 'Romanticism is an excess of emotion'. And Eliot concurs: 'excess of emotion', he writes, '(which is surely a fault)'.

By describing himself as a 'classicist in literature', Eliot means he was an anti-romantic and therefore against 'excess of emotion'. A cancelled digression from Eliot's essay 'The Function of Criticism' is straightforwardly useful here. The passage in question can be found in the original publication of the essay in *The Criterion* (October 1923). There, Eliot clearly distinguishes, *fundamentally* distinguishes between the romantic position and the classicist position. He writes: 'the romantic is deficient or undeveloped in his ability to distinguish between fact and fancy, whereas *the classicist, or adult mind, is thoroughly realist*—without illusions, without daydreams, without hope, without bitterness, and with abundant resignation' [my italics]. Add to this Eliot's assertion in '*Ulysses*, Order and Myth' (1923): 'I think that Mr Aldington and I are more or less agreed as to what we want in principle, and agreed to call it classicism.'

To summarise: Eliot's letter to the *TLS* in 1920 finds the polarity of 'classicism' and 'romanticism' unhelpful; but he deplores 'excess of emotion' and identifies that excess with 'romanticism'. By 1923, he identifies 'classicist' with 'realist'—and embraces 'classicism' in principle.

To this evidence, we can add even earlier documentation, thanks to Ron Schuchard's tireless research. In September 1916, Eliot had been married for a year, his father had discontinued his allowance, and Eliot mollified his worried parents by completing his Harvard doctoral thesis on F. H. Bradley the philosopher. He also had to find money and did so by lecturing on modern French and English literature at Oxford and London. The prospectus for Eliot's extramural, or extension, course in 1916 for six lectures on modern French literature is arranged around the idea of Romanticism and the opposition to it, Classicism: 'contemporary intellectual movements in France must be understood as in large measure a reaction against the "romanticist" attitude of the nineteenth century.' Eliot's potential students learned that 'Romanticism stands for *excess* in any direction'. The germ of all these tendencies, Eliot writes, can be found in Rousseau—especially the 'emphasis upon *feeling* rather than *thought*' and the 'depreciation of *form* in art, and the glorification of *spontaneity*'. In *The Monist* (April 1918), Eliot wrote: 'To be in love with emotion has been our affliction since Rousseau.'

Also useful is Eliot's wary editorial, 'The Idea of a Literary Review', in January 1926. It was written for the relaunch of *The Criterion* as *The New Criterion*. Eliot was leery of programmes and platforms, but here he is prepared to identify a 'modern tendency'. But it is a tendency which, he warns, is likely to be imprecise and personal. 'I believe that the modern tendency is towards something which, for want of a better name, we may call classicism . . . there is a tendency—discernible even in art—toward a higher and clearer conception of Reason, and a more severe and serene control of the emotions by Reason'. Eliot then mentions some key texts. *But*, as an explanation for his preferred use of the word 'tendency', he emphasises the theoretic divergencies of these key texts. They are *Réflexions sur la violence* by Georges Sorel, *L'Avenir de l'intelligence* by Charles Maurras, *Belphégor* by Julien Benda, *Speculations* by T. E. Hulme, *Réflexions sur l'intelligence* by Jacques Maritain, and *Democracy and Leadership* by Irving Babbitt.

The keynote here is '*a more severe and serene control of the emotions by Reason* [my italics]'.

The obvious objection to this theory of Eliot's poetic—as classicist and anti-romantic—is that his declaration of classicism is made in 1928, when half of his greatest poetry has already been written. The examples and declarations I have just cited from 1920, 1923, and 1926 go some way to answering this objection. As does the prospectus of 1916 for six lectures on modern French literature.

There are several other answers to be advanced against the idea that the poetry precedes the interest in classicism. Obviously, conviction and poetic and critical practice can precede public declaration of principles. Although Eliot clearly hadn't read *Belphégor* until July 1920—and is writing to Pound: 'I recall his name as a colleague of Péguy'(3 July 1920)—Benda is in a French critical tradition whose thrust is recognisable and familiar to Eliot. At Harvard, he attended Irving Babbitt's course 'Literary Criticism in France'. And he would have read Babbitt's *Masters of Modern French Criticism* (1912). Obviously, there are variants and minor disagreements within this tradition. They are recorded, indeed made much of, in P. Mansell Jones's *Tradition and Barbarism*—a study of classicism's dossier against Romanticism that Eliot commissioned for Fabers in 1930. But classicism's fundamental direction and disposition remain unchanged. It is, looked at broadly, the realist tradition and its key text could be said to be Flaubert's *Madame Bovary*.[5] In English, *Mrs. Bovary*—pointedly prosaic, though never so translated.

In 'Dante' (1929), Eliot complained that 'a great deal of sentiment has been spilt, especially in the eighteenth and nineteenth centuries, upon idealising the reciprocal feelings of man and woman towards each other, which various *realists* have been irritated to denounce.' [my italics] As a group, the modernists were eager to co-opt science to their anti-romantic agenda. In 'Tradition and the Individual Talent', Eliot deployed an analogy taken from a chemical catalyst when speaking of poetic composition. In *Stephen Hero*, Joyce invoked science: 'the modern spirit is vivisective.'[6]

I want to address now another objection to the definition of classicism as opposition to excess emotion. It is that Eliot frequently states that emotion is the artist's primary material. 'What every poet starts from is his own emotions', he writes in 'Shakespeare and the Stoicism of Seneca' (1927). There, Eliot belittles the role of philosophy in poetry. Dante has the 'advantage' of an 'orderly and strong and beautiful' philosophy—that of Aquinas—and Shakespeare the 'disadvantage' of an inferior current of thought. But neither 'advantage' nor 'disadvantage' matters—because the *sine qua non*, 'the essential is that each expresses, in perfect language, some permanent human impulse'.

This might sound romantic in orientation, but it is Eliot the classicist, Eliot the subtle connoisseur of feelings, sifting the fugitive from the febrile, the oddly genuine from the overstated and conventional, who writes in the same essay: 'In reality there is precise emotion and there is vague emotion. To express precise emotion requires as great intellectual power as to express precise thought.'

The other factor in Eliot's classicism is the poetry of Jules Laforgue. Eliot recorded many tributes. In 1908, he encountered *The Symbolist Movement in Literature* by Arthur Symons: 'but for having read his book, I should not, in the year 1908, have heard of Laforgue or Rimbaud; I should probably not have begun to read Verlaine, I should not have heard of Corbière.' In 'What Dante

Means to Me' (1950) he delivered another forthright tribute to Laforgue: 'Of Jules Laforgue I can say that he was the first to teach me how to speak, to teach me the poetic possibilities of my own idiom of speech.' In 'To Criticise the Critic' (1961), Eliot returned to his debt: 'I have written about Baudelaire, but nothing about Jules Laforgue, to whom I owe more than to any one poet in any language.'[7]

These fulsome acknowledgements have puzzled readers of the *Collected Poems*, where 'Conversation Galante', 'Mr. Apollinax', and perhaps 'Rhapsody on a Windy Night' are generally thought to be the only sustained Laforguean exercises in Eliot's poetry in English,[8] though there is a scattering of verbal echoes in other poems. The publication of *Inventions of the March Hare* emphatically confirmed the imperiously edgy presence of Laforgue in Eliot's work. There, Laforgue is almost omnipresent—in his diffident, self-effacing way. And not simply in the early suppressed poetry. On the first draft A of 'Whispers of Immortality', Eliot typed: 'the first two lines of the fifth verse wont [*sic*] do, they are conscious, and exhibit a feeble reversion to the Laforgue manner.' The *manner* is arch, pointed, self-conscious—*mannered*. Its heft, its steer, its direction is something else—something fundamental to Eliot's poetic programme.

In Laforgue's poetry, emotion is comically excessive and undermined by overstatement. Its inclination is classicist. Laforgue partly invents the antiheroic, wry, realistic note of modern poetry. In England, his counterpart is Clough—another poet highly regarded by Eliot—whose Claude, in *Amours de Voyage*, 'doutait de tout, même de l'amour'. Laforgue's tone is ironically self-dramatising, inconveniently prosaic, febrile and flat-footed, ruefully bathetic, comically accurate. It avoids poetry's weakness for eloquence or indulges it ironically. Passion is invariably punctured. Sometimes the dregs, trace elements, homeopathic quantities of authentic emotion remain.

Eliot's comic poems, which are indebted in varying degrees to Laforgue, tend to be sidelined by criticism. They are worryingly lucid in a culture trained to prize the 'defining' obscurity of modernism. (The exception is 'Mr Eliot's Sunday Morning Service', a humoresque in which the ironic mandarin lexis is comically at odds with its familiar, weekly subject matter: spotty adolescents with their coins for the collection plate become the 'pustular' young 'clutching piaculative pence'.) And the comic poems are anomalous in a poetic oeuvre commonly characterised as displaying crepuscular profundity. One way of coping with the anomalous is to misread it, as Eliot noted in 'Shakespeare and the Stoicism of Seneca': 'I am used to having cosmic significances, which I never suspected, extracted from my work (such as it is) by enthusiastic persons at a distance.'

'The *Boston Evening Transcript*' is a tiny masterpiece of comedy. It turns very simply and brilliantly on the gross hybridity of the verse—the awkward conflation of the poetic and the irredeemably, thumpingly prosaic. It is tonally axiomatic that the three words '*Boston Evening Transcript*' are clunky. Here they function like a leg iron on a gnat. No sooner is the poem airborne than it is grounded.

Eliot's model here is Arnold's bathetic deployment in *Culture and Anarchy* of another newspaper's name. With the withering ironic banter of which he is master, with feigned credulity, Arnold's prose pretends to an ever greater precision, which is actually rhetorical inflation awaiting the final tin-tack of irony. 'The word, again, which we children of God speak, the voice which most hits our collective thought, the newspaper with the largest circulation in England, nay, with the largest circulation in the whole world, is the *Daily Telegraph!*"

Of the nine lines in Eliot's poem, three end with the fatally flat title, the *Boston Evening Transcript.* But this analysis doesn't quite do justice to the comic variety within the initial grid. That grid is established immediately in the radical disjunction between the first two lines, the immovable pedestrianism of the opening line, and the irresistible melodic pastoral of the second line:

> The readers of the *Boston Evening Transcript*
> Sway in the wind like a field of ripe corn.

The beauty of the second line proves to be gimcrack, of course, because the line means that the readers go whichever way the wind blows. (In his early period, particularly in the lighter verse, Eliot plays wittily with cliché.) The bulk of the poem thereafter is a single, long sentence—a vain attempt to achieve syntactical momentum doomed to end in the bathos of the *Boston Evening Transcript.* Actually, this effect is doubled. After the initial run-ins with the *Boston Evening Transcript* in the title and first line, we twice more encounter it. Before the first of these, there are three clauses: a pentameter, another pentameter with an anacrusis, and an arrhythmical thirteen-syllable line. I mention the rhythm pedantically because its contribution to the comedy is crucial:

> When evening quickens faintly in the street
> Wakening the appetites of life in some
> And to others bringing the *Boston Evening Transcript,*

But on the second of these occasions, the sabotage is even greater because the preliminaries are more extensive. Before the fourth and final *'Boston Evening Transcript'*, there are four lines in which the regular rhythmic pulse fights for survival and fails—first locally, then, finally, comprehensively:

I mount the steps and ring the bell, turning
Wearily, as one would turn and nod goodbye to
La Rochefoucauld,
If the street were time and he at the end of the street,
And I say, 'Cousin Harriet, here is the *Boston Evening*
Transcript.'

At the previous count, there were thirty-four syllables preceding the *'Boston Evening Transcript'*. Here there are a pentameter, a sixteener, a thirteener, and a final eleven syllables: a total of fifty syllables. It is the poetic equivalent of a long sprint down a cinder track, ending in the no-jump of the *'Boston Evening Transcript'*. The comedy is delicious, and identifiably Laforguean.

Where poetry tends typically to reach for afflatus, in Laforgue its affinities are with the pratfall. 'Aunt Helen' is Eliot's great comically subversive anti-elegy. Its prim, even archaic tone—'Cared for by servants to the number of four'—is at odds with the anarchic elements of misrule we witness. The first line is a perfectly regular iambic pentameter: 'Miss Helen Slingsby was my maiden aunt.' It is succeeded by sustained metrical irregularity: 'He was aware that this sort of thing had occurred before' must be the least singing line in the history of English poetry—poker-faced, pedestrian, wordy. There are, too, irregularities of other kinds—sexual indiscretions which are described methodically, soberly even, so that the orgiastic implications remain an innuendo. It may be a mild indiscretion for the footman to have the second housemaid on his knees. But Eliot insinuates—using only the words 'on' and 'upon'—a busier spectral promiscuity of people and things: the Dresden clock is on the mantelpiece, the footman is upon the dining table, and the second housemaid on his knees. Despite the cool tones, the scene is sticky with contact.

There are sly underminings throughout the poem. If Miss Slingsby is 'cared for', it is only by servants. 'Now when she died there was silence in heaven / And silence at her end of the street.' That 'now', with its conversational tone, immediately undercuts the grandeur of 'there was silence in heaven', which recalls the 'silence in heaven about the space of half an hour' after the opening of the seventh seal in Revelations (8:1)—making available to the reader two competing ideas. Which are, silence in heaven as a mark of universal respect and silence in heaven as a mark of theological indifference. The ironic damage is continued and concluded in the bathetic 'silence at *her end* of the street'. Not the entire length of the street, then—just her end of it. The tonal reticence of 'But shortly afterwards the parrot died too' is crackling with mischief. Eliot delivers his bathos with the *gravitas* of a Jeeves.

So, a funny poem, yet one with the poetic courage to take the elegy and empty it of conventional sentiment, while ironically preserving its surface proprieties. One thinks of *In Memoriam* XX, where Tennyson discusses grief in hierarchical terms, using the metaphor of servants in a house where the master has died:

Who speak their feeling as it is,
And weep the fulness from the mind:
'It will be hard,' they say, 'to find
Another service such as this.'

The servants' grief here is sincere enough, but temporary, and tinged with allowable self-interest. So Tennyson is himself discriminating soberly among the varieties of grief—the great theme of *In Memoriam*. But he doesn't have Eliot's mischievous, modernist cynicism. He hasn't read Laforgue. He isn't a classicist mistrustful of the obvious emotions—those standard, strong emotions that every one will admit to, but which very few actually experience, except impurely.

On 18 July 1919, Richard Aldington, after first praising Eliot's critical prose, concluded: 'I feel compelled to add that I dislike your poetry very much; it is over-intellectual and afraid of those essential emotions which make poetry.' Quite so. Substitute 'obvious' for 'essential' and the staleness of Aldington's narrow preference is clear. Eliot the modernist, Eliot of the classicist 'tendency', was interested in a wider range of emotions, portrayed more precisely.

Not necessarily recherché emotions, but rather emotions which are declared, implicitly, to be unsuitable for poetry by the torpid consensus. What is the emotion in 'Mr. Apollinax'? When you consider its brilliant, off-kilter, almost Byronic comic rhymes— 'unbalanced'/'challenged'; 'Channing-Cheetah's'/'foetus'—you might easily think there is little room for emotion. But it is there. It is there in the discomfiture of Mrs. Phlaccus and the Channing-Cheetahs. It is there in the intellectual vanity, the *esprit d'escalier*, of '"There was something he said that I might have challenged"'. It is above all there in the narrator's undisguised glee at the general discomfiture. These are interesting emotions—glee, bafflement, vanity, malice—common enough in life, rarely sighted in poetry.

Intellectual passion—another emotion almost designed, you might think, to provoke Aldington—isn't an easy subject for a poet. Wordsworth brings it off when he describes Newton's bust in book

3 of the 1850 *Prelude* as 'The marble index of a mind for ever / Voyaging through strange seas of Thought, alone'. Eliot's physical equivalents are quirkier, comic, decorous, and indecorous. On the one hand, the niceties of intellectual discrimination are modestly present—their objective correlative is the tinkle of laughter 'among the teacups' and the evocation of 'shy' (and aptly named) Fragilion. On the other hand, consider the objective correlative of passion and revelation *in impropria persona* with Priapus—gaping, ambiguously, 'at the lady in the swing'. Eliot does not specify whether Priapus is 'staring', or 'open-mouthed', or if his fly is open.[9]

The poem is often said to be about the philosopher, Bertrand Russell, in America. Perhaps. Russell taught Eliot, was his mentor in England, shared his flat with the newly marrieds, aided him financially, and cuckolded him. Russell was a man who, in his person, conflated unruly passions and categorical imperatives. He might be Eliot's model for Mr. Apollinax—even though the poet later reserved some of his most mordant remarks for Russell and his 'enervate gospel of happiness', whereas here the tone is warmly, generously amused. As the epigraphs from Lucian's *Zeuxis* make clear: 'What novelty', 'by Hercules, what paradoxes', and 'What an inventive man'. 'How on earth does he think of such things?' the quotation continues.

The quickness of Mr. Apollinax's mind is suggested by the fluent, elusive stream of metaphors and similes, describing his comic metamorphoses: Fragilion, Priapus, a foetus, the old man of the sea, a centaur. His name suggests he may be the son of Apollo and therefore tinged with inspiration—a quick-change artist whose interlocutors can scarcely keep up.

'Mr. Apollinax' is a poem about the unsettling effect of laughter—and a set of variations on laughter. Mr. Apollinax *laughs his head off*: 'I looked for the head of Mr. Apollinax rolling under a chair.' He *curls up with laughter*: 'He laughed like an irresponsible foetus.' His *waves of silent laughter* are directed at his companions who are *out of their depth*—two ordinary enough ideas that are transformed by Eliot's great linguistic gifts into an image of disconcerting beauty: 'His laughter was submarine and profound / Like the old man of the sea's / Hidden under coral islands / Where worried bodies of drowned men drift down in the green silence, / Dropping from fingers of surf.' It is partly the incomparably judged fifteen-syllable line—whose extended horizontal stands for depth—which makes this epic simile work. But it is even more the adjective 'worried'. It functions like the adjective 'irresponsible' applied to a foetus. Both are not only surprising, out of left field, unpredictable: they are, in fact, inappropriate. The drowned are beyond worry. The foetus may be innocent, but that isn't the same thing as 'irresponsible'. But because the two adjectives are so bizarre, they seem carefully chosen and therefore carry extra conviction. William Burroughs exploits the same effect in his titles, *The Naked Lunch* and *The Ticket That Exploded*. Or compare Sylvia Plath's 'Sun struck the water like a damnation', from her poem 'Suicide off Egg Rock'—which is what Nabokov called 'an unattached comparison'. As a technique, it locks in the reader's hermeneutic impulse.

The allusion to the centaur is harder to interpret. We have Mr. Apollinax's conversation, 'his dry and passionate talk', with its double valency, paradoxically cool *and* heated—and the hybrid centaur is a neat equivalent. Of course, there are other possible readings of the centaur: the idea of *horseplay* (compare Yeats's 'On a Picture of a Black Centaur by Edmund Dulac' (1928): 'I knew that horseplay, knew it for a dangerous thing'). Perhaps it is appropriate that the reference should be Greek to us—unintelligible—since Mr. Apollinax outpaces everyone:

> Of dowager Mrs. Phlaccus, and Professor and Mrs. Cheetah
> I remember a slice of lemon, and a bitten macaroon.

A witty, wounding collocation, this—bizarrely memorable nomenclature and a visual memento of amnesia. The signifier floating free of the signified. But this is a poem in which meaning liquefies and clichés change shape like smoke, before the blunt bathos of that bitten macaroon.

Another poem about laughter, Eliot's prose poem, 'Hysteria' (1915), has provoked its own share of hysteria. In it, a male speaker describes being engulfed by his female companion's hysterical laughter and the waiter's attempt to save the situation by moving the couple outside. Accusations of coldness and misogyny have been levelled against the poem. Coldness may seem a plausible charge, but it is a fatally partial account of 'Hysteria', which is, in fact, about one of the most powerful emotions known to man—embarrassment. Not an emotion Aldington would identify as suitable for poetry, but one most people have suffered. Eliot himself more than most. (In 1922 the Bel Esprit charitable scheme set up to help him financially, was supposed to free him from debilitating employment at Lloyds Bank. Eliot felt belittled by the charity. The embarrassment caused by the deteriorating Vivien dates from 1920 onwards: in 1930 Virginia Woolf described Vivien as 'this bag of ferrets ... Tom wears round his neck'. In 1915, however, 'Hysteria's date of composition, the newly married couple were happy.)

Another misjudged reading is that the mental disturbance isn't taking place in the woman but in the man. This seems a wilful misreading. After all, the 'trembling hands' of the elderly waiter suggest that even a marginal participant recognises there is something peculiar taking place, objectively, *en plein air*, and not in the man's mind, hence the waiter's anxiously repeated suggestion of rustication.

On the other hand, 'Hysteria' exemplifies what Eliot identified (a mite eccentrically) as the 'unpleasantness of great poetry' in Blake. Stephen Medcalf was alluding to this tendency when, in the *Times Literary Supplement* (7 June 1996), he floated the idea of a punk Eliot[10]—bent on shocking his readers out of their poetic preconceptions. Sid Vicious and Johnny Rotten don't seem obviously Eliotean analogues, but Medcalf has a point, even if he overstates it. 'Hysteria' is shocking still, whereas we have long ago decided to smile indulgently at the publicity tactics of the Sex Pistols and their successors.

In 'Hysteria' and 'Dans Le Restaurant' (April 1917), restaurant poems both, the private (what we really feel) obtrudes into the public sphere. This same collision is repeated in 'Sweeney Erect' (1919), where the woman's pitilessly observed epileptic fit is heard outside in the corridor. The 'ladies of the corridor'—not tarts, but fussing and respectable inhabitants of a boarding house— observe 'that hysteria / Might easily be misunderstood', a sentiment unlikely to be voiced by working prostitutes. Sweeney is indifferent. He continues shaving and discounts the fit as 'female temperament'. The peripheral figures in these poems, 'the ladies of the corridor' and the 'elderly waiter', are vital because they provide an audience. Without an audience, embarrassment is void and merely potential.

Eliot is writing about our *dislike* of displays of strong emotion—hysteria, 'female temperament'. He is writing about cold embarrassment. Unpleasant, yes, but recognisable, if we are honest, as what we *really* feel.

'Hysteria' is a drama of involvement and detachment, shaped like a sonnet with a versus, or turn. 'As she laughed I was aware of becoming involved in her laughter and being part of it, until her teeth were only accidental stars.' If the woman's teeth are stars, the speaker is inside, in the dark—utterly and unwillingly sucked in, 'lost finally in the dark caverns of her throat'. And the reader is inside, too, with the speaker.

Involvement is replaced by detachment, triggered when the waiter intervenes. There is a move from internal to external: 'An elderly waiter with trembling hands was hurriedly spreading a pink and white checked cloth over the rusty green iron table.' The table is 'rusty' because it is outside—so the psychological shift in the speaker is mirrored in the physical move outside the restaurant. The speaker's point of view is now objective, detached. He is not interested in *why* the woman is laughing hysterically. We, too, no longer *hear* the laughter or experience it intimately: we see it in 'the shaking of her breasts'. It is like a silent film. And it is as if it is happening to someone else, not to the speaker, or to us. And this is a true emotion—what Keats called 'the feel of not to feel it' and what Emily Dickinson, another great anatomist of the emotions, pinpointed when she wrote about the experience of trauma, 'A doubt if it be Us / Assists the staggering Mind . . . '.

'Hysteria' encapsulates an emotional contradiction, the contradiction that is embarrassment, and it does so with precision. In *Howards End*, Forster writes, quasi-paradoxically, of 'panic and emptiness'. The feelings described by Eliot the modernist, Eliot the classicist, are more radically incompatible. We see total immersion *and* fastidious detachment. We see the sudden shift from viscera ('the dark caverns') and incongruous imagery to controlled linguistic irony—from 'stars with a talent for squad-drill' to the wry, saving comedy of applying 'careful subtlety', not to a philosophical crux, but to rampant craziness. Here, the shaking of someone's breasts presents itself as the problem and the 'solution' is concentration and 'careful subtlety'. The myth of mind over matter has seldom looked less plausible—particularly since it is someone else's matter.

'Dans Le Restaurant' further illustrates Eliot's modernist interest in incompatible emotions. It is, you could say, about conflicting reactions to the dilapidated waiter—a combination of indifference shading into tedium, frank disgust, and the unexpectedly visionary. The poem describes the maundering of an old waiter recalling an unrealised sexual episode from his childhood, when he was seven years old. In a sense, it is also a poem that touches on the idea of the failure of feeling. 'Between the desire / And the spasm' comes, not the Shadow, as in *The Hollow Men*, but a dog: 'Il est venu, nous peloter, un gros chien; / Moi j'avais peur, je l'ai quittée à mi-chemin' [A big dog came, pawing us. I was afraid; I stopped half way].

The tedium visited on his customer by the waiter is manifest as the bored client tots up the stains on the waiter's waistcoat: 'Les taches de son gilet montent au chiffre de trente-huit' [the stains on his waistcoat reached a total of thirty-eight]. The disgust erupts as the waiter reaches the climax—the anticlimax—of his reminiscence: 'Va t'en te décrotter les rides du visage; / Tiens, ma fourchette, décrasse-toi le crâne' [Go and get the mud off the wrinkles in your face; / here, my fork, give your skull a good clean out]. The waiter's grubbiness is emblematic of his inner filth and the customer responds with the French equivalent of 'Wash your mouth out with soap and water': 'Tiens, voilà dix sous, pour la salle-de-bains.' [Here, ten cents, to go to the baths.]

The coda, however, is freighted with pathos, noble with loss— and later becomes the 'Death by Water' section of *The Waste Land*: 'Phlébas, le Phénicien, pendant quinze jours noyé, / Oubliait les cris des mouettes et la houle de Cornouaille.'[Phlebas the Phoenician, fifteen days drowned, forgot the cry of seagulls and the Cornish swell.] Finally, the speaker concedes—more than concedes, is *stricken*, pierced by the knowledge that this dismal destiny ('un sort pénible') was once, however, a beautiful man of tall stature: 'Cependant, ce fut jadis un bel homme, de haute taille.' But we fail. As in 'Prufrock', 'Human voices wake us and we drown.' Our beginnings ('un bel homme') never know our ends (a waiter with a fat arse, 'à la croupe arrondie', absently but unforgettably scratching his fingers).

In *The Use of Poetry and the Use of Criticism* (1933), Eliot demolishes Arnold's poetic pretensions by jeering at Arnold's complaint (to Clough) that the age was 'unpoetical': 'no one can deny that it is of advantage to a poet,' Arnold argued, 'to deal with a beautiful world'. Eliot is sceptical: 'the essential advantage for a poet is not, to have a beautiful world with which to deal: it is to be able to see beneath both beauty and ugliness; to see the boredom, and the horror, and the glory.' As a poetic prescription, this directive is sounding, orotund rather than obviously practicable—and calculated to exceed Arnold's reach.

The focus of our attention should be on the impossibility of Eliot's imperative—those obviously incompatible, contradictory requirements , 'the boredom, and the horror, and the glory'. Impossible in strict logic, perhaps, but psychologically realisable—realised, in fact, in 'Dans Le Restaurant', whose tedium, disgust, and touch of the visionary fulfil Eliot's prescription of boredom, horror, and glory.

In chapter 21 of *Lord Jim*, Conrad writes: 'very few of us have the will or the capacity to look consciously under the surface of familiar emotions.' It is this modernist, classicist programme that animates Eliot's poetry and is candidly avowed in 'Religion and Literature' (1935): '[Knowing what we like] means knowing what we really feel: very few know that.'

In 'Dans Le Restaurant' the speaker experiences a cacophony of conflicting emotions and the waiter exemplifies the inexplicable ontological fissure between the beautiful beginning and the ugly end.

The speaker of 'Journey of the Magi' (1927) is also surprised by the counterintuitive emotions he experiences when he witnesses the birth of Christ: 'I had seen birth and death / But had thought they were different; this Birth was / Hard and bitter agony for us, like Death, our death.' Of course, as a group, the Ariel poems describe the collision of beginnings and ends; a theme that Eliot begins with 'Portrait of a Lady' ('But our beginnings never know our ends!') and concludes with *Four Quartets* ('In my beginning is my end'). As well as inaugurating this preoccupation with beginnings and ends, 'Portrait of a Lady' concludes with its callow, cocksure speaker not only disconcerted for once, but also emotionally confounded: '*Not knowing what to feel* or if I understand / Or whether wise or foolish, tardy or too soon . . . ' [my italics]. The poem shows Eliot's abiding preoccupation with mixed feelings—in this case, the shift from distant amused conde-scension at the *salonista* to a rueful sense of another person's frail quiddity.

I HAVE CONSIDERED ELIOT'S POETRY from two perspectives, two po-tentially contradictory perspectives. The first is Eliot's abiding sense that life is often a failure to live fully—to have a proper, vivid, satisfying emotional life. And I have explained that this yearning for fulfilment is almost a cliché of romanticism—but comes to Eliot from Henry James, a prophylactic source, from an author so 'mer-cilessly clairvoyant', in Eliot's striking encapsulation, that the theme is divested of the conventional and the simple. This is James's preface to *What Maisie Knew*, outlining the role of his young heroine, Maisie: 'To live with all intensity and *perplexity* and felicity in its terribly mixed little world would thus be the part of my interesting small mortal' [my italics].

The other counterperspective is implicit in that James quotation—which, even as it extols intensity, insists on complexity. The clas-sicist in literature is sceptical of strong emotion as a virtue in itself. Eliot's most sustained exposition of the classicist position is in *After Strange Gods* (1933): 'it is a cardinal point of faith in a ro-mantic age, to believe that there is something admirable in violent emotion for its own sake.' Again: 'many people act upon the as-sumption that the mere accumulation of "experiences", includ-ing literary and intellectual experiences, as well as amorous and picaresque ones, is—like the accumulation of money—valuable in itself.' What follows from this unexamined conviction is the downgrading of art, the downgrading of form. Instead, there are competing individual belief systems: 'a serious writer may sweat blood over his work, and be appreciated as the exponent of still one more "point of view".' Writing is judged by its doctrine, by its disposition, rather than by its art.

Is it possible to reconcile the desire 'to live with all intensity' with the distrust of 'violent emotion for its own sake'? Clearly, Eliot was aware of the tension between the two positions—the one 'romantic', the other 'classicist'. 'My friend Dr. Paul Elmer More is not the first critic to call attention to an apparent incoherence between my verse and my critical prose . . . It would appear that while I maintain the most correct opinions in my criticism, I do nothing but violate them in my verse.' Eliot's answer is that 'in one's prose reflexions one may be legitimately occupied with ideals, whereas in the writing of verse one can only deal with actuality'.

There is a better answer, if one uses his poetry as exemplary. But this option was not available to Eliot, whose modesty forbade the use of his public platform to analyse and explain his own poetry. Living 'with all intensity', for Eliot, as for Henry James, is to complicate life's readied simplifications. It is to be one of James's 'super-subtle fry'—a morally fastidious Fleda Vetch, rather than a coarsely pragmatic Adela Gereth, in *The Spoils of Poynton*; *The Ambassadors*'s Lambert Strether, *The Golden Bowl*'s Maggie Verver. All of them scrupulous, disinterested, and self-effacing. And the best illustration of this is the comic, antiromantic creation, J. Alfred Prufrock, who fails to make a proposal of marriage, and yet isn't a dullard, but a thin-skinned sensitive—a dithering compass of cowardice and crippling lack of self-esteem. Prufrock fails to live, fails to declare himself—and is therefore culpable by romantic lights. He does not seize the day. But he isn't simply a moral coward. His motives and emotions are neither theatrical nor exaggerated. They are complicated, subtle, divided, and partially occluded from himself. Which is a classicist take on his predicament. The classicist sifts, tests, and discriminates among his emotions. So Prufrock fails to 'live', fails to act on his powerful, repressed, buried romantic feelings—because they are in conflict with his emotional scruples, a tragicomic wariness, a profound amorous modesty.

And this conflict is, paradoxically, a very intense form of living: 'I have measured out my life in coffee spoons.'

Obviously, the protomodernist Laforgue makes a contribution, but so does Browning. 'The Love Song of J. Alfred Prufrock' (1911) is a dramatic monologue—though one that, unlike Browning's typical scenario, flinches away from the moment of crisis, with its maximal potential for self-revelation. Of course, the comic touches of surrealism, the sudden glitches in focus—for instance, 'restless nights in one-night cheap hotels' is a memory, not the route it apparently purports to be—these things are largely foreign to Browning. Nevertheless, the whole poem looks much more traditional than it once did. Even Eliot's opening avant-garde trump—the evening 'like a patient etherised upon a table'—is a recognisable variation on the sunset troped as blood. Compare Maupassant's *Une Vie*: 'The sun, lower now, seemed to be bleeding.' Or Mayakovsky's 'The Cloud in Trousers': 'again they've beheaded the stars, / And the sky is bloodied with carnage'.

The verse itself, often inaccurately described as 'free', is actually strewn with rhymes and is mostly iambic, or iambic for long stretches: 'And I have known the eyes already, known them all— / The eyes that fix you in a formulated phrase, / *And when I* am formulated, sprawling on a pin, / When I am pinned and wriggling on the wall, / Then how should I begin / To spit out all the butt-ends of my days and ways? / And how should I presume?'

The italicised words are the only ones that present us with an aural ambiguity, created by the extra syllable 'And'. The rest is iambic. No wonder e e cummings, reviewing *Prufrock and Other Observations* in *The Dial*, should have singled out for praise Mr. Eliot's 'skilful and immediate violins'.

In 'What Dante Means to Me' (1950), Eliot declares that he wanted to 'establish a relationship between the medieval inferno and modern life'. His example, however, is taken from *The Waste Land* and the parallel doesn't apply to 'Prufrock'—despite its references to disturbing the universe (a hyperbole for the social order) and to Lazarus returning from the dead (another, comic, hyperbole for something important, a matter of life and death). If there is a parallel with Dante, it is in the opening line, 'Let us go then, you and I'—which, given Eliot's epigraph from the *Inferno*, conceivably summons Dante and his guide, Virgil. More plausibly, the line could be simply addressed to the reader.

More important here is the co-presence of Marvell's 'To His Coy Mistress'. 'To have squeezed the universe into a ball / To roll it towards some overwhelming question' inevitably calls up Marvell's 'Let us roll up all our strength, and all / Our sweetness, up into one ball'—and, therefore, the whole idea of carpe diem, the traditional answer to 'the failure to live'. Here, though, the imperative is addressed not to the sexually reluctant woman. For once, quirkily, it is the man who is failing to seize the day.[11]

This is partly because Prufrock is clearly at a social disadvantage. Though he is correctly dressed in a morning coat, he is nervous about a great many things—eating, for one. At the end of the poem, presumably uncertain about the correct method, he asks, 'Do I dare to eat a peach?' Near the beginning, it is the fear of being faced with a unfamiliar dish that absolutely confounds him:

'And time for all the works and days of hands / That lift and drop a question on your plate.' Prufrock is panicked by 'the eternal Footman', too—'eternal' here meaning 'inevitable' or 'usual' rather than anything supernatural. Think of the butler in *Little Dorrit* who intimidates his employer, Mr. Merdle. Eliot's way of expressing this panic is at once literal ('And, in short, I was afraid') and in the form of a surreal analogue: 'Though I have seen my head (grown slightly bald) brought in upon a platter . . . '

Lest we think this impossibility is literally true, we have Prufrock's disclaimer: 'I am no prophet—and here's no great matter.' It is simply an elaborate way of saying he has 'lost his head'. A periphrasis of genius, revivifying a cliché; compare Eliot's four deadly sins in 'Marina' or Mr. Apollinax laughing his head off.

Something else, though, apart from social disadvantage, apart from the sense that salon conversation about Michelangelo might be difficult to sustain, is hampering Prufrock's amorous conviction. It is partly because he is uncertain that his inclinations will be reciprocated: perhaps the woman may respond with 'That is not what I meant at all. / That is not it at all'. Thus far, Prufrock is psychologically cognate with the upper-class Claude of Clough's *Amours de Voyage*. There is another, darker reason for Prufrock's Hamlet-like procrastination, however.

'Then how should I begin / To spit out all the butt-ends of my days and ways? / And how should I presume?' That he is presuming—getting above himself socially—is axiomatic. But it doesn't explain the vein of self-disgust in the poem, a self-disgust that marks Prufrock off from his prototype in *Amours de Voyage*. What are 'the butt-ends' of his 'days and ways'? What does the metaphor signify? It is confessional ('to spit out' something) and sordid ('butt-ends'). Part of Prufrock feels unworthy, an unworthiness he articulates only indirectly: 'Shall I say, I have gone at dusk through narrow streets / And watched the smoke that rises from the pipes / Of lonely men in shirt-sleeves, leaning out of windows? . . . ' Is this meant to invoke a fellow feeling, a kinship with the lonely? Or is it less innocent? Why 'at dusk'? Why 'narrow streets'? The next two lines contribute, in their oblique, imagistic way, to clarification: 'I should have been a pair of ragged claws / Scuttling across the floors of silent seas.' We don't need Golding's *Pincher Martin* to remind us that the predatory and the crab are a plausible link. The crab here is reduced to the metonymic grasping part. Think of Eliot's brilliantly desolate account of sex in 'Whispers of Immortality', 'To *seize* and *clutch* and penetrate' [my italics]. There is something on Prufrock's conscience, something at the periphery of articulation—something that is clearer but also coarser in Eliot's judiciously suppressed 'Prufrock's Pervigilium', which describes a trawl through a red-light district in *Inventions of the March Hare*. (The title glances at the medieval *Pervigilium Veneris*, the watch night of Venus or the night vigil of love.)

Prufrock feels physically inadequate ('how his arms and legs are thin!'), socially disadvantaged, nervous, romantically charged, reluctant to imperil a relationship—and physically impure. So, he fails to act. He fails to live. But the tortured intensity, the reluctance, with which he feels these several, complex emotions give meaning to the line, 'I have measured out my life with coffee spoons'—which is not the declaration of simple triviality it is often assumed to be,[12] but a triviality imbued with Jamesian tragic intensity, equal to the last, deceptive, heartbreaking sentence of *Washington Square*: 'Catherine, meanwhile, in the parlour, picking up her morsel of fancy-work, had seated herself with it again—for life, as it were.' For the rest of her life. Instead of life. Has the worn qualifier, 'as it were', ever been made to do so much? In both cases, Catherine Sloper and Prufrock, behind the simplicity of romantic disappointment, there are rich, complex emotions—*classicist* emotions. On the one hand, a Jamesian failure to live. On the other, a Jamesian complexity of causation.

So complex, in fact, that the protagonist finds clarity too difficult: 'It is impossible to say just what I mean! / But as if a magic lantern threw the nerves in patterns on a screen.' Imagine, Prufrock proposes, that his inner life were visible, even though he finds it impossible to articulate lucidly. This is Arnold's 'The Buried Life': 'Alas! Is even love too weak / To unlock the heart and let it speak? / Are even lovers powerless to reveal / To one another what indeed they feel?' In many ways, we are dealing here with a cliché of the nineteenth-century Zeitgeist—roughly equivalent to the twentieth-century modishly perverse platitude that language is always an obstacle to expression. Compare, for example, the idea of moral isolation as we find it in chapter 3 of Dickens's *A Tale of Two Cities* (1859):

> A wonderful fact to reflect upon, that every human creature is constituted to be that profound secret and mystery to every other ... In any of *the burial-places* of this city through which I pass, is there a sleeper more inscrutable than its busy inhabitants are, in their innermost personality, to me, or than I am to them? [my italics]

The difficulty of introspection is also articulated by George Eliot in book 2, chapter 17 of *Adam Bede*: 'it is a very hard thing to say the exact truth, even about your own immediate feelings—much harder than to say something fine about them which is *not* the exact truth.' On her honeymoon, Jeanne, in Maupassant's *Une*

Vie, has an epiphany: 'for the first time she realised that two people never penetrate each other's souls or the depths of each other's thoughts. They walk side by side, sometimes clasped close, but they never mingle and each one's moral being remains eternally isolated.' This idea of moral opacity survives in Waugh's *Brideshead Revisited*. Mrs. Stuyvesant Oglander professes, on the slightest acquaintance, to know Ryder 'through and through'. Ryder reflects: 'Can you indeed see into those dark places where my own eyes seek in vain to guide me?' The idea reaches its decadence in Tennessee Williams's preface to *Cat on a Hot Tin Roof*: 'As a character in a play once said, "We're all of us sentenced to solitary confinement inside our own skins."'

In 'Prufrock', Eliot is drawing on the idea of the buried life and Arnold's poem—which argues that our inner life is hidden, not just from others, but from ourselves. We don't know what we really feel: 'But hardly have we, for one little hour, / Been on our own line, have we been ourselves— / Hardly had skill to utter one of all / The nameless feelings that course through our breast, / For they course on forever unexpressed.' This is both a romantic position: we are failing to live, because we are not in touch with our deepest selves. And it is a classicist position: our emotions are so complex they are beyond us and below us. Eliot, as is well known, alludes to 'The Buried Life' in 'Portrait of a Lady' ('My buried life, and Paris in the Spring'). Yet the version Eliot prefers is the philosophised version of *The Waste Land* note, which refers us to F. H. Bradley's *Appearance and Reality*: 'every sphere is opaque to the others which surround it.'[13] He prefers Bradley's exposition for two reasons: its expression is drier, philosophical, more persuasive because less poetic; Bradley allows Eliot to disguise a debt to Arnold, his irritating father-figure.

Bradley's argument, in actual fact, is less radical than this quotation makes it seem. Bradley did not believe that individuals were trapped in their own private worlds, martyrs to inescapable solipsism: 'what, however, we are convinced of, is briefly this, that we understand and, again, are ourselves understood.'[14] His position is the unassailable one that we have no immediate, direct access to the minds of other people. However, though there is no mental telepathy, there are physical means by which we can communicate our thoughts and feelings. He means language and speech—the sounds we make with our vocal cords, or the gestures and signs we make if we are unable to speak or hear: 'souls affect each other, in fact, only through their bodies, but we insisted that, none the less, the ideal identity between souls is a genuine fact.'[15] I'm not sure Eliot understood this.

Arnold proposes something much more radical than Bradley and necessarily unprovable: the idea that our inner lives are buried, inaccessible to us, or only intermittently accessible. This is Eliot in his 'Conclusion' to *The Use of Poetry and the Use of Criticism* (1932–1933): '[Poetry] may make us from time to time a little more aware of the deeper, unnamed feelings which form the substratum of our being, to which we rarely penetrate; for our lives are mostly a constant evasion of ourselves, and an evasion of the visible and sensible world.' It is this idea, the idea of the buried life, 'the substratum of our being', that Eliot elaborates in *The Waste Land*.

Why else would it begin with 'The Burial of the Dead'?

Three

THE WASTE LAND

ELIOT'S GREAT POEM, written when he was only thirty-four, begins with 'the buried life', with a literal version of the general proposition: 'Winter kept us warm, covering / Earth in forgetful snow, feeding / A little life with dried tubers.' This is followed by a demonstration of 'the buried life'—in fact, a *series* of demonstrations.

Confronting Eliot's mesmeric opening words, 'April is the cruellest month', critics commonly cite Chaucer's 'General Prologue', but Tennyson's *In Memoriam* (CXVI) is nearer in spirit: 'Is it, then, regret for buried time / That keenlier in sweet April wakes . . .' (Particularly since Tennyson's *Maud* is the source for 'a handful of dust'. The mad narrator in an asylum thinks he is dead: 'And my heart is a handful of dust'.[1] Or, rather, *buried alive*: 'why have they not buried me deep enough?')

Eliot's general proposition is that 'April is the cruellest month', because what was thought dead is painfully brought to life. Plant life ('breeding / Lilacs out of the dead land') quickly succumbs to pathetic fallacy ('mixing / Memory and desire'). The nonhuman segues swiftly into the human—and the human speaking voice, *a human speaking voice*: 'Summer surprised us, coming over the Starnbergersee / With a shower of rain; we stopped in the colonnade, / And went on in sunlight, into the Hofgarten . . . '

How should one characterise this voice? By acknowledging the appropriateness of Eliot's original section title, 'He Do the Police in Different Voices', a quotation from Dickens's *Our Mutual Friend* that describes Sloppy reading the newspaper to Mrs. Higden. The voice is brittle, reminiscing, gushing, confident, cosmopolitan, unforgettable, echt, alive in the ear. Eliot impersonates its foreign inflections, imposes them authoritatively on us. The voice is loud and clear. Then it is gone.

To be replaced by another undeniable voice, the prophetic voice (of Tiresias): 'Son of man, / You cannot say, or guess, for you know only / A heap of broken images . . . ' The voices are so differentiated it might be opera—tenor, baritone, bass, contralto, soprano. And then it *is* opera, *Tristan und Isolde*, briefly: '*Frisch weht der Wind / Der Heimat zu* . . . ' Then Wagner's is replaced by another voice, ' "They called me the hyacinth girl".' And that by another: 'Fear death by water. / I see crowds of people, walking round in a ring. / Thank you. If you see dear Mrs. Equitone . . . '

(Only a very great poet would risk the brilliant banality of 'thank you'. How much those two worn words establish—not gratitude, but reflex gratitude, the trite elision of prophecy with payment, a bathetic zeugma. Madame Sosostris, the medium in 'The Burial of the Dead', is a tabloid Tiresias.)

The poetry is seeded with a clue to Eliot's purpose here. Madame Sosostris evokes 'Belladonna, the Lady of the Rocks'. That is, the *Mona Lisa*, Leonardo da Vinci's portrait, sometimes known as *La Gioconda*. In a famous essay in *The Renaissance*, Pater wrote that 'she is older than the rocks among which she sits'. Unmistakably, then, Madame Sosostris is summoning 'the young third wife of Francesco del Giocondo' when she summons 'the Lady of the Rocks'. And Eliot, in his turn, is summoning Pater's notorious rhapsody on Leonardo's painting. There, Pater attributes to the picture the philosophy of previous existences, or metempsychosis: 'like the vampire, she has been dead many times.' 'The fancy of a perpetual life,' Pater writes, 'sweeping together ten thousand experiences, is an old one'. He is shrewd enough to offer a modern take on this old idea: 'modern philosophy has conceived the idea of humanity as wrought upon by, and summing up in itself, all modes of thought and life.' In its way, this is an evolutionary version of Eliot's aesthetic, the relationship between tradition and the individual talent: the new thing is a development, a continuation, of all that has gone before.

In fact, the idea of metempsychosis is central to *Ulysses*, the modern novel Eliot most admired—'the most important expression which the present age has found'.[2] Metempsychosis is itself a variant on the idea of the buried life. What is buried within us that resists access? Answer: in this case, previous lives—voices that suddenly speak, and buttonhole us before they are suddenly gone.

Critics have puzzled over what Eliot meant by 'Stetson! / You who were with me in the ships at Mylae!' The apostrophe isn't a puzzle at all. Eliot expects us to take it literally—as evidence of the interlocutor's and the speaker's previous lives. The reference to Baudelaire is equally unmysterious: 'You! Hypocrite lecteur!— mon semblable,—mon frère!' This is the last line of Baudelaire's 'Au Lecteur'. Here it is a proclamation of identity ('mon semblable') with the reader. Yet the shared identity is a shared doubleness. As

well as meaning 'hypocritical', the adjective 'hypocrite'[3] in French
has connotations of dissimulation, of concealment—in fact, of 'the
buried life', the hidden inner self.

The idea of previous lives, a multiplicity of lives, is explicit in
Eliot's over-helpful, essential, yet extraneous and aesthetically
illegitimate note explaining the hermaphroditic Tiresias, 'throb-
bing between two lives'. Actually, a great many more than two:
'the most important personage in the poem, uniting all the rest.
Just as the one-eyed merchant, seller of currants, melts into the
Phoenician Sailor, and the latter is not wholly distinct from
Ferdinand Prince of Naples, so all the women are one woman,
and the two sexes meet in Tiresias.' Without this note—an ex-
trinsic appendage—the reader could eavesdrop on Eliot's Babel
of voices, but it would be impossible to fathom his organising
rationale. Given this collective unconsciousness, these pooled
personalities, these jumbled genders, we gradually become
aware that *The Waste Land* is predicated on an implicit, unstated
assumption—the simultaneity of time.

In his famous essay, '*Ulysses*, Order and Myth' (1923), Eliot
credited Joyce with the invention of an ironic method for dealing
with the formlessness of modern life—the use of an organising
myth. This method, Eliot wrote, 'has the importance of a scien-
tific discovery'. It is 'a continuous parallel between contempor-
aneity and antiquity'—which 'is simply a way of controlling, of
ordering, of giving a shape and a significance to the immense pan-
orama of futility and anarchy which is contemporary history'. Eliot
adapts Joyce's 'discovery' in *The Waste Land*—past and present
are not arranged in orderly ironic parallel, where one has priority.
Rather, past and present displace each other in a series of disrup-
tive exfoliations. In *Ulysses*, mythic antiquity nourishes but never

usurps the twentieth-century narrative of Leopold Bloom. In *The Waste Land*, however, we hear a clamour of separate voices, suddenly focused, and just as suddenly silent. There seems to be no obvious hierarchy. As in *The Adventures of Augie March* (1953), 'first to knock, first admitted'. For example, in 'The Fire Sermon', the three Thames daughters ('Down Greenwich reach / Past the Isle of Dogs') double and alternate with the Rhine maidens' vocalese from *Götterdämmerung* ('Weialala leia / Wallala leialala'). Queen Elizabeth and the Earl of Leicester are evoked with subtle eroticism—'beating', 'stern', 'swell', 'White towers'— and then displaced by the drably clamant voices of the successive Thames daughters. Though they are separate, the story they tell is a continuity—from a joyless seduction ('I raised my knees / Supine on the floor of a narrow canoe'), through an erotic postmortem on an infidelity ('He promised "a new start"'), to a sense of shame and social inferiority ('My people humble people who expect / Nothing'). Their story in summary is trailed at the opening of 'The Fire Sermon': 'The nymphs are departed. / And their friends, the loitering heirs of City directors; / Departed, have left no addresses.'

The narrative liquefactions here are mirrored in the conclusion of 'A Game of Chess' where Eliot consciously emulates the bravura notation of the realistic, endless, but endlessly differentiated goodnights in Joyce's 'The Dead': 'Goonight Bill. Goonight Lou. Goonight May. Goonight. / Ta ta. Goonight. Goonight. / Good night, ladies, good night, sweet ladies, good night, good night.' From a local pub in London, Eliot suddenly transports his readers to Denmark and the deranged Ophelia. 'HURRY UP PLEASE IT'S TIME' is, then, not only the publican's cry at closing time. It is also a way of compacting chronology—of making the sequential simultaneous. And how clever of Eliot to give his female cockney predator the perfectly plausible contemporary line: 'You ought to be ashamed, I said, to look so *antique*' [my italics]. Compare the recently evoked 'antique mantel'. In a single word— reeking of East End vernacular and of the classical world—Eliot collapses time.

In *The Waste Land: A Facsimile and Transcript*, the idea of previous lives, of reincarnation, of buried lives, is explicit in Eliot's invocation, later excised, of the Buddhist Wheel of Rebirth, *Samsara*: 'London, your people is bound upon the wheel'; 'The inhabitants of Hampstead are bound forever on the wheel'. Of course, this wheel didn't survive to the final version. But 'The Fire Sermon' refers us to the Buddha's sermon at Uruvela and Madame Sosostris deploys 'the Wheel' as part of her predictions. Eliot's involvement with Buddhism is better acknowledged now than it was when I first drew attention to its structural import in 1973. Here, one quotation, from *Notes towards the Definition of Culture* will suffice: 'I know that my poetry shows the influence of Indian thought and sensibility.' (For further documentation, see my reprinted 1973 essay, '*The Waste Land*', in *Haydn and the Valve Trumpet*, 1990.)

Why the waste land, the desert, as a central symbol? The head-note to *The Waste Land* acknowledges the crucial contribution of Jessie L. Weston's *From Ritual to Romance*: 'Not only the title, but the plan and a good deal of the incidental symbolism of the poem were suggested by Miss Jessie L. Weston's book on the Grail legend.' And yet, in 1956, in 'The Frontiers of Criticism', Eliot disowned this note, deploring the way he had 'sent so many enquirers off on a wild goose chase after Tarot cards and the Holy Grail'.[4]

In fact, though, Eliot's poem can't be read properly without basic knowledge of the Grail myth and the rudiments of *From Ritual to Romance*—which guide the structural plot of *The Waste Land*, though not to the intricate, esoteric degree envisaged by Grover Smith's reading. The argument of Jessie L. Weston's *From Ritual to Romance*—implicit in its title—is that the Grail story is a transformation of, an outgrowth from, older vegetation rituals.[5] Her strategy, then, follows Frazer's *The Golden Bough*, which is also acknowledged in Eliot's notes.

In other words, *the Grail story itself has a buried life.*

Thus, the Fisher King is the impotent ruler of an infertile land. The curse can only be lifted with the arrival of a stranger who can put or answer certain ritual questions. In the Grail legend, a knight searches for the cup used by Christ at the Last Supper. The knight journeys to the Chapel Perilous where he must put certain questions about the Grail—after which the plight of the land is cured.[6] In the vegetation ceremonies, the image or effigy of the fertility god is thrown into the sea to symbolise the death of summer, without which spring could not follow. The crucifixion and resurrection of Christ are assimilated to these traditions.

In brief, Eliot travesties this template on occasion and transforms it on others. The ritual questions, for example, are assimilated to the fable of the thunder from the *Brihadaranyaka Upanishad*: '*Datta*: what have we given?' In the Grail legend, a choir of children sing at the foot-washing ceremony that precedes the restoration of Anfortas by Parsifal. In Eliot's poem, the ceremony is a vulgar burlesque:

O the moon shone bright on Mrs. Porter
And on her daughter

They wash their feet in soda water

Et O ces voix d'enfants, chantant dans la coupole!

Phlebas the Phoenician, a trader interested in profit and loss, is drowned in 'Death By Water'—aping the drowning of the fertility god's effigy. The Chapel Perilous is 'the empty chapel' of 'What the Thunder Said'.

At the same time, we haven't left London—one of several 'unreal' and interchangeable cities. We are seeing it under surreal conditions. St. Mary Woolnoth's striking bell, which has 'a dead sound on the final stroke of nine', recurs transmogrified in part V as 'towers / Tolling reminiscent bells, that kept the hours'. In part I, St. Mary Woolnoth also 'kept the hours'. Likewise, the hysteric woman of 'A Game of Chess' reappears in 'What the Thunder Said'. Originally, her brushed hair 'Glowed into words'. In part V, 'A woman drew her long black hair out tight / And fiddled *whisper* music on those strings' [my italics]. One thinks of the Degas model whose long hair provides the strings for the cello of her naked body, whose comb is the bow. The 'golden Cupidons' are now 'bats with baby faces'—a sinister variation[7] perhaps cognate with the madness of 'Hieronymo's mad againe' in Eliot's fragmentary finale.

Eliot's coinage, 'Unreal city', owes a great deal to Buddhist ideas of *maya* or illusion. Later it is assimilated to the Christian idea of this fleeting world. In *Murder in the Cathedral*, the chorus refers to Hebrews 13:14: 'for here we have no continuing city, but we seek one to come.' Or, in Eliot's play: 'Here is no continuing city, here is no abiding stay.' Religions have a way of slighting the temporal.

In 1971, I attended a brilliant lecture in Oxford by Christopher Ricks. It dealt with tone in Eliot's poetry, particularly *The*

Waste Land. Twenty years later, it became part of *T. S. Eliot and Prejudice*. A member of the audience detected something peripheral, even evasive, in Ricks's dazzling attention to detail—and asked if she might ask Ricks what he thought *The Waste Land* was *about*. Ricks referred her to the latest Walter Matthau movie, *Charlie Varrick*, in which a crop sprayer turned bank robber uses his crop-sprayer's licence to buy some dynamite. As Charlie Varrick is negotiating the door, encumbered by a brown paper grocery bag full of TNT, the salesman speaks: 'May I ask you what that dynamite is for?' Varrick smiles and leaves his answer hanging in the air: 'You may.'

But the 'meaning' of *The Waste Land* is clear enough. We need only glance ahead to Eliot's 1934 morality play, *The Rock*. Of course, there will always be local difficulties, impacted cruces, uncertain transitions, but the central focus is clear: 'you neglect and belittle the desert. / The desert is not remote in southern tropics, / The desert is not only around the corner, / The desert is squeezed in the tube-train next to you, / The desert is in the heart of your brother.' The desert is a candid, recognisably familiar symbol for spiritual aridity, for the failure of feeling. A few years on, Auden's ballad 'As I Walked Out One Evening' exploits the same topos: 'The desert sighs in the bed.' By the simplest expedient—merely avoiding the word 'desert' and substituting 'the waste land'—Eliot masks the obvious, disguises the drift of his central symbol.

One should never underestimate actual experience in the making of poetry. John Hayward wrote to Eliot on 1 August 1941 about a draft of *Little Gidding*: ' "Autumn weather": I do not get the significance of *autumn*? It struck me as having a greater significance than you may have intended it to have.' Eliot replied on 5 August 1941: ' "Autumn weather" only because it *was* autumn weather . . . ' The kingfisher in *Burnt Norton* turns out to be a reminiscence of a kingfisher Eliot saw in the summer of 1935 at Kelham. In the same way, the churches mentioned in *The Waste Land* are all churches threatened with demolition, whose preservation Eliot was campaigning for.[8]

As an American by birth and a sentimental agrarian by disposition, Eliot was probably drawn to the emblematic potential of the waste land because he had actual experience of ecological disaster—desolation that he reports en passant in *After Strange Gods*, as I explain overleaf. From Wordsworth and Wordsworth's poetic heir Arnold, Eliot inherited the theme of a rift between man and his natural surroundings. 'The world is too much with us; late and soon, / Getting and spending, we lay waste our powers: / Little we see in Nature that is ours', Wordsworth lamented, just as Hopkins was to deplore, in 'God's Grandeur', a world 'smeared and bleared with trade'. Arnold's 'The Forsaken Merman' is an allegory of the rift between man and nature—the unresponsive woman in the grey church, the pleading merman. The merman is metonymic of the pagan world that Wordsworth had also (guardedly) lamented: 'Great God! I'd rather be / A Pagan suckled in a creed outworn; / So might I, standing on this pleasant lea, / Have glimpses that would make me less forlorn; / Have sight of Proteus rising from the sea; / Or hear old Triton blow his wreathèd horn.'

This theme, this elegiac ruralism, is prominent in *Inventions of the March Hare*, Eliot's early, unpublished poetry. Vacant lots in 'Second Caprice in North Cambridge' are emblematic—'helpless fields that lie / Sinister, sterile and blind'. The next poem, 'Interlude in London', portrays city dwelling as a form of hibernation 'among the bricks', 'Indifferent to what the wind does'. 'Easter: Sensations of April' again shows an asphalt world with perturbing trace elements of nature—a red geranium, daffodils, and the odour of earth.

1933 was a year of intense literary activity for Eliot. He was barely off the podium. He gave the Turnbull lectures at Johns Hopkins, the Charles Eliot Norton lectures at Harvard, and the Page-Barbour lectures at the University of Virginia. (He also delivered lectures at UCLA, New York, Buffalo, Princeton, Pasadena, Yale, Smith, Bryn Mawr, Vassar, and Mount Holyoke: the list of names seemingly ready for a railroad conductor's rapid recitation.) In *After Strange Gods*, his 1933 lectures delivered in Virginia, Eliot begins by praising 'the agrarian movement in the South', 'the neo-agrarians', and their quixotic belief in a return to preindustrial rural culture nurtured by 'opulent soil'. Eliot ruefully records the landscape seen on his journey from Montreal to New England—a mixture of misguided clearance methods and industrialism. 'The forest was razed to make sheep pastures for the English settlers; now the sheep are gone, and most of the descendants of the settlers'; then 'the sordor of the half-dead mill towns of southern New Hampshire and Massachusetts'. Eliot sums up by invoking the desert: 'those New England mountains seemed to me to give evidence of a human success so meagre and transitory as to be more desperate than the desert.'

The desert and the great dust bowl storms were to come in the 1930s, of course, but the American Eliot was aware of the soil erosion caused by the Homestead Acts of 1862 and 1909. The 1862 Act gave 160 acres of land to settlers for a ten-dollar filing fee and five years residence. The 1909 Enlarged Homestead Act increased the acreage to 320. It was a disastrous policy, fatally tied to the new railroad. The railroad needed immigrant settlers, attracted by the prospect of free land, because it needed customers.

The railroad, however, followed the riverbeds for obvious ease of construction—and the railroad companies, therefore, owned the fertile land. The infertile land on offer to settlers was higher up, far from the railroad.

To persuade sceptics, therefore, there was a theory that 'rain follows the plough', that any human activity created rainfall. One railway firm, the Santa Fe Railroad, maintained that a 'rainline' was advancing at the rate of eighteen miles a year. A popular, evangelical manual, *Campbell's Soil Culture* by Hardy W Campbell, promised that intense cultivation of the soil conserved moisture. Farmers were being told to pulverise the topsoil: 'I will show you fear in a handful of dust.' The ecological disaster—culminating in the 1930s dust storms—was already in train. A poem such as Frost's 'The Census-Taker', written before 1923, describes the very landscape Eliot was to see on his later journey from Montreal—'an emptiness flayed to the very stone', created by deforestation, which Frost, like Eliot, calls a 'desert'.[9]

If we know now what *The Waste Land* 'means', the poetry still hoards its surprises, much as Stravinsky's *Rite of Spring* retains its power to shock. In his *The Use of Poetry and the Use of Criticism*, his Charles Eliot Norton lectures at Harvard in 1932–1933, Eliot had this to say about poetic meaning:

> The chief use of the 'meaning' of a poem, in the ordinary sense, may be . . . to satisfy one habit of the reader, to keep his mind diverted and quiet, while the poem does its work upon him: much as the imaginary burglar is always provided with a bit of nice meat for the house-dog.

I invoke the *Rite of Spring* deliberately because *The Waste Land* presents its readers, its *auditors*, with a revolutionary sound world.

And sound *world* is exact here. Eliot's poem glows with international potential, like one of those old-fashioned radios with a glowing menu of stations—from Hilversum and Stockholm, to Karachi and Delhi. Consider the climax:

London Bridge is falling down falling down falling down
Poi s'ascose nel foco che gli affina
Quando fiam uti chelidon—O swallow swallow
Le Prince d'Aquitaine à la tour abolie
These fragments I have shored against my ruins
Why then Ile fit you. Hieronymo's mad againe.
Datta. Dayadhvam. Damyata.
  Shantih shantih shantih

In sequence, Eliot gives us an English nursery rhyme, Dante's *Purgatorio*, the late antiquity Latin text *Pervigilium Veneris*, Tennyson's 'The Princess' (section IV, the Prince's song), Gerard de Nerval, Kyd's *Spanish Tragedy*, and the *Upanishads*. Thematically, this is a Babel of voices from buried lives—the next supplanting the one before, so that *'Quando fiam uti chelidon'* [when shall I be like the swallow] skips a few hundred years from the *Pervigilium* to Tennyson's swallow. Aurally, the range of registers here introduces us to the auditory equivalent of the Silk Road and the spice trail. The exotic is in our mouths and in our ears—delicious tastes, pungent sound bites. Eliot is a great cartographer of the ear's outbacks and jungles and ancient ruins. His ear is famished for novelty. Like Keats, he has an ear 'open like a greedy shark'—for the new tidbit and the faint tingle of the old.

No wonder, then, that his account of the auditory imagination, in *The Use of Poetry*, should also be an account of the buried life of language: 'the feeling for syllable and rhythm, penetrating far below the conscious levels of thought and feeling, invigorating every word; sinking to the most primitive and forgotten, returning to the origin and bringing something back, seeking the beginning and the end.'

'O O O O that Shakespeherian Rag' is an example of that fusion. Like a classical composer, Stravinsky say, using jazz idioms, or Olivier Messiaen using the marimba, or John Adams hearing the connection between Schönberg's atonality and the Looney Toons cartoon music, Eliot welds the high and the low. On the one hand, in 'A Game of Chess' there is a sumptuous pastiche of Enobarbus's speech in *Antony and Cleopatra*—a triumph of evanescent syntactic sinuosity, calculated inversion ('coloured glass / Unstoppered') and the flamboyantly absent main verb. The passage is all profusion without sensuality. It is a simulacrum only. On the other hand, there is the trammelled cockney from the pub, indebted to Kipling's innovatory *Barrack Room Ballads*: 'It's them pills I took to bring it off, she said.'

Perhaps because the sex is frequently squalid and therefore untitillating, we do not register now what a radical departure, in its inclusion of sex, *The Waste Land* was. Compton McKenzie's *Sinister Street* had been shocking—though its sexual daring now looks homeopathic. So had Lawrence's *Women in Love. Ulysses* was banned. And here is Eliot, *in a poem*, touching on Mr Eugenides's proposition ('a weekend at the Metropole'), rape ('so rudely forc'd'), a *boffe de politesse* ('unreproved, if undesired'), and the desolate factuality of 'I raised my knees', which has all the eroticism of 'I raised the blinds'.

I think Eliot writes acutely about sex—in all its variety. He does accurate justice to the variety of its disappointments. Like D. H. Lawrence, he is alive to the nugatory sexual experience. And like

Lawrence, too, he is equally true to the terror and transfiguration of the naked encounter: 'blood shaking my heart / The awful daring of a moment's surrender.' If sex can be trivial, it can also be overpowering and daunting. We are schooled, programmed to think of sex as a 'normal' part of life. It takes a poet as great as Eliot to displace this impoverished stereotype, to remind us that the erotic can be overwhelming, its wonder awash with terror:

> I could not
> Speak, and my eyes failed, I was neither
> Living nor dead, and I knew nothing,
> Looking into the heart of light, the silence.

In his Dante essay of 1929, Eliot provides us with a gloss on this experience, strangely divided between ecstasy and the sense of extinction:

> the experience of a poem is the experience both of a moment and of a lifetime. It is very much like our intenser experiences of other human beings. There is a first, or an early moment which is unique, of shock and surprise, even of terror (*Ego dominus tuus*); a moment which can never be forgotten, but which is never repeated integrally; and yet which would become destitute of significance if it did not survive in a larger whole of experience, which survives inside a deeper and calmer feeling.

We all know the cliché—falling in love—but it takes an Eliot to record the vividness of its vertigo.

And everywhere there is Eliot's unsleeping linguistic alertness and his properly opportunistic detail: the 'unshaven' Mr Eugenides's 'demotic French' and his 'pocket full of currants'; Tiresias's droll pedantic cod-precision ('And I Tiresias have foresuffered all / Enacted on this same divan *or bed*' [my italics]); 'the *dusty* trees' [my italics] (brilliantly retrieved from an early unpublished poem, 'First Debate between the Body and Soul'), which speak so eloquently of summer in the city; the canopy of leaves over the river ('the river's tent'). And what are we to make of 'the *lean* solicitor' [my italics] made palpable by a single, irrefutable adjective?

Consider, too, the beating pulse in these two adjacent, cunningly unpunctuated, present participles: 'the human engine waits / Like a taxi throbbing waiting.' Note also the ironic reminiscence of Keats's 'Ode to a Nightingale': Eliot's 'Out of the window perilously spread / Her drying combinations touched by the sun's last rays' nodding facetiously to Keats's 'Charmed magic casements, opening on the foam / Of perilous seas in fairy lands forlorn'.

The Waste Land is Eliot's greatest dramatic work.

Its voices make a relished cacophony—competing, dominating, jostling, assertive, irrefutable, gone. The single, acutely differentiated voices in Browning's dramatic monologues—the radical idiolects of Caliban, Blougram, Karshish, Sludge—provide Eliot with his exempla, but *The Waste Land* is his fragmented and anonymous *The Ring and the Book*. Browning's great long poem is made from the monologues of six named characters and three anonymous voices, 'Half-Rome', 'The Other Half-Rome' and 'Tertium Quid'. Its purpose is to re-create a particular historical passage in all its evanescent detail, for which Browning uses the image of a firework—brilliant but hasting 'to blend with black!' Eliot's purpose, in 433 lines, is to re-create history itself, via his swarming largely anonymous voices.

The one voice we do not hear is Eliot's.

There is a problem about Eliot's voice. Unlike many poets, Eliot is a poet of voices: the controlled, yet faintly querulous voice of Prufrock; the desiccated voice of Gerontion. Isaiah Berlin divided thinkers in hedgehogs and foxes. The hedgehog is the thinker with one major idea that he curls around, envelopes, and fosters, like Karl Marx and his analysis of the contradictions within capitalism. The fox is the thinker with many ideas. Eliot the poet is thematically a hedgehog—excavating the (for him) inexhaustible mine that is the buried life. Stylistically, he is, like Picasso, a fox—an artist with many styles, all of them Eliotean, all of them bearing his signature. Consider the callow superiority of the voice of the young man in 'Portrait of a Lady', before he gets his comeuppance and is disconcerted by the older woman's unlooked-for frankness. Or the detached, cool, aesthetically complacent speaker of 'La Figlia Che Piange', who is also disturbed and involved in the girl's pain, despite himself. Neither speaker is Eliot. They and their voices are characterised—subtly but unmistakably.

We first encounter Eliot's own voice in *Ash-Wednesday* ('Because I do not hope . . . ') and later in *Four Quartets* ('So here I am, in the middle way, having had twenty years— / Twenty years largely wasted, the years of *l'entre deux guerres*'). In the other earlier poetry, there *is* a voice which is neither dramatic and characterised nor imbued with Eliot's own tones; it is a neutral, toneless voice, which he deploys to great effect. It is without personality. It is impersonal. Accurate, lucid, almost mathematical, the voice of record, fastidious in its choice of words: 'Phlebas the Phoenician, a fortnight dead, / Forgot the cry of gulls, and the deep sea swell / And the profit and loss.' This voice is part of Eliot's extraordinary power as a poet—and an inadvertent vindication of the theory of impersonality.

We are used to writers with a verbal style: Bellow's hybrid of high culture and gutter garrulity; Robert Lowell's plangent, iambic throb; Marianne Moore's art of pernickety elaboration and qualification. We often feel uneasy about writers without a strong verbal stylistic signature. Sometimes, apparently, we believe that style is primarily a verbal construct—a matter of lexis, taxis, imagery, rhythm. Inferior writers patent a few verbal oddities—think of e e cummings and his wearisome faux-naïveté. But true style is ultimately a way of seeing, of thinking. A great writer like Milan Kundera leaves us with an overwhelming sense of his style—even though we read him in translation in English, and he writes in Czech or French.

You might think *The Waste Land*'s opening employs Eliot's own voice: 'April is the cruellest month.' But it is quickly made obvious that the speaker is one of the buried: 'Winter kept *us* warm . . .' [my italics] Nor is Eliot the 'I' of the line, 'I had not thought death had undone so many'—which is a quotation from Dante's *Inferno*, canto III. Sometimes the 'I' is Tiresias, sometimes the Fisher King. A personal appearance in the poem by Eliot—like one of Alfred Hitchcock's furtive cameos in his movies—would introduce a consistent aural element into a work whose method is aural surprise and vocal unpredictability. It is crucial to Eliot's prestidigitation that there should be no stable register, no consistent *point de repère*. Occasionally, very occasionally, Eliot's neutral, impersonal, objective voice is heard. But it is also true to say that in *The Waste Land* Eliot's subject is not himself but the buried life itself—in history, in religion.

You might say that his method was to uncover layer after layer, to excavate buried lives, to archaeologise myth from conflated myth—were it not that these voices erupt without regard to chronology. *The Waste Land* takes place in a permanent present tense. It is, in Pound's phrase, news that stays news. An omnipresent.

Four

FOUR QUARTETS

Four Quartets (1943) is Eliot's last poetic work. The quartets were written from 1936 to 1942. The first, *Burnt Norton,* grew out of lines in *Murder in the Cathedral* and first appeared in *Collected Poems 1909–1935.* This was followed by *East Coker* in 1940, *The Dry Salvages* in 1941, and *Little Gidding* in 1942. The definitive account of their genesis can be found in Helen Gardner's *The Composition of Four Quartets.* Initially, the early quartets were received with a certain scepticism, a scepticism sometimes bound up with dislike of Eliot's Christianity and his perceived orthodoxy. (In fact, Eliot's religious writings demonstrate the angularity and awkwardness, the unbiddable intransigence of sincere belief.) George Orwell, for one, thought Eliot's early poetry had been diluted by Christianity and the requirement, as he put it— alluding to Lewis Carroll's *Alice's Adventures in Wonderland*—to believe ten impossible things before breakfast. Since then, other commentators have wrinkled their noses at the candidly prosaic nature of some of the verse—and even wondered, in one case, if Eliot was writing *deliberately* badly. Actually, Eliot is consciously addressing the problem of register in the long poem—and the need to vary it. *Four Quartets* is as radical as anything he wrote.

Its subject is time and the mystical experience.

The simultaneity of time—*The Waste Land*'s covert, yet blatantly deployed hypothesis—is explicitly expounded in *Four Quartets*.

This is the deliberately abstract, deliberately dry beginning of *Burnt Norton*, an opening of careful reservations and persuasively undramatic tones and acoustic. We are in the lecture room, listening to the noise of chalk on the blackboard and the unhurried expository voice [my italics]:

> Time present and time past
> Are both *perhaps* present in time future
> And time future contained in time past.
> *If* all time is eternally present
> All time is unredeemable.

To redeem something means to recover or retrieve it. Here Eliot argues that you cannot *get something back* if it is 'eternally present'. So, by 'unredeemable', Eliot effectively means 'unchangeable'. At the end of this section, those modifiers ('if' and 'perhaps') have been suppressed: 'Time past and time future / What might have been and what has been / Point to one end, which is always present.' Such a view of time follows logically, inexorably, from the idea of an omniscient God—whose omniscience necessarily entails knowing the future, as Calvin's concept of predestination was ready to acknowledge.

As a way of explaining the imminent appearance of Saxons and other figures in Eliot's historical pageant, *The Rock* (1934) the idea of simultaneous time had already been coarsely expounded by Bert/Ethelbert. The eerily accurate cockney of *The Waste Land* has now become the standard substandard caricature: 'There's some new notion about time, what says that the past—what's be'ind you—is what's goin' to 'appen in the future, bein' as the future 'as already 'appened. I 'aven't 'ad time to get the 'ang of it yet; but when I read about all those old blokes they seems much like us'.[1]

Eliot's problem, the problem of *Four Quartets*, is the problem of the mystical experience—which by definition takes place outside of time, both conventional, linear time and simultaneous time. Eliot had already trailed this idea in *Murder in the Cathedral*, in which Becket admits the murderous knights to the cathedral with the words: 'It is not in time that my death shall be known; / It is out of time that my decision is taken / If you call that decision / To which my whole being gives entire consent.'

Because time is an omnipresent, it cannot be changed. However, though mystical experience takes place outside of time, it can only be remembered in time: 'To be conscious is not to be in time / But only in time can the moment in the rose-garden, / The moment in the arbour where the rain beat, / The moment in the draughty church at smokefall / Be remembered.' In his 1931 essay on Pascal, Eliot observed that 'even the most exalted mystic must return to the world, and use his reason to employ the results of his experience in daily life'.

Eliot, like Pascal, is not a mystic—although 'what can only be called mystical experience happens to many men who do not become mystics'. In *Four Quartets*, he remakes the tradition of religious mystical poetry in English. By the early twentieth century, the old tradition of jewelled vision—'The Dream of the Rood', *Pearl*, Richard Rolle—is a titter of trinkets, robbed of eloquence by over use. Not only is the mystical idiom threadbare, Eliot is also writing when science is beginning to assert its intellectual hegemony wider than the world of the Royal Society. Think of Eliot's conjuring of the mathematician Lobatchevsky in his Jonson essay in *The Sacred Wood*: 'It is a world like Lobatchevsky's: the worlds created by artists like Jonson are like systems of non-Euclidean geometry.' Even in the rarefied and somewhat depleted world of *The Family Reunion*, mention is made of the 'Heaviside layer'—an indication of the way science had penetrated social life beyond the laboratory.

Hence the professionalised air, the microdistinctions, the quasi-scientific abstractions of Eliot's opening to *Burnt Norton*. We feel we are in a world of reservations, 'restricted to What Precisely, / And If and Perhaps and But'—the pedantic world of 'How Unpleasant to Meet Mr. Eliot', rather than the genuinely uncertain mystical ambience of 'If and Perhaps and But' that we are about to enter. Language is about to become porous, paradoxical, elastic, shifty, shifting, contradictory, intelligently perverse. Twenty years earlier, in his essay on the metaphysical poets, Eliot wrote that sometimes it was necessary for a poet 'to dislocate if necessary, language into his meaning'. In *Burnt Norton* section V—the fifth section of each quartet is given over to self-conscious literary reflection—Eliot expresses the same idea, though with a more pessimistic tinge to his argument:

> . . . Words strain,
> Crack and sometimes break, under the burden,

Under the tension, slip, slide, perish,
Decay with imprecision, will not stay in place,
Will not stay still.

Long before Jacques Derrida coined the term 'deconstruction'—
to define language's semantic indeterminacy, its insoluble, inevitable and *diametric* ambiguities—Eliot was using its slippage very consciously and precisely to create a linguistic formula equal to describing something that takes place out of time, yet can only be remembered in time:

Footfalls echo in the memory
Down the passage which we did not take
Towards the door we never opened
Into the rose-garden. My words echo
Thus, in your mind.

Here we have two sentences that liquefy under the weight of their qualifications, in which the narrative momentum is weighed against its clear negation—not once ('which we did not take') but twice ('we never opened'). Paradoxically, the negatives themselves attain a positive force as we discover that their negative status cannot prevent the progress of the sentence. Willy-nilly, the reader has gone down a passage towards a door, opened it, and found himself in the rose-garden. Noise is crucial here. Noise contributes its reality effects—an otiose piece of jargon usually, but perfect and precise in this context. First there is the echoing noise of footfalls, which immediately becomes the memory of an echo. This echo is conflated with Eliot's words as they echo in the mind.

The idea of memory is repeated implicitly in the image of potpourri, rather than real roses: 'But to what purpose / Disturbing the dust on a bowl of rose-leaves / I do not know.' Potpourri is a memory of fresh roses—and also an echo of roses, a diminished repeat.

So far, there are five echoes: the echo of footsteps, the remembered echo of footsteps, the echo of words, the echo of words in the mind, and dried roses as an echo of roses.

Eliot continues his echoic theme: 'Other echoes / Inhabit the garden.' At first, we think of ordinary echoes among this plethora of echoes and the uncertainty they create. Then we assess the word 'inhabit'—an unusual verb, suggesting residence; a slightly awkward verb, where 'throng' or 'sound' would be more readily acceptable. Acceptable, were it not for the fact that gardens do not echo. An echo requires acoustic conditions—in particular, confinement, hard surfaces to trap sound and reflect it—that a garden does not supply. And, in any case, these echoes have a kind of permanence. They *inhabit* the garden.

They. 'There *they* were.' 'There *they* were as our guests.' 'And *they* were behind us.' 'So we moved, and *they*, in a formal pattern.' Who are 'they'? Grammatically, they can only be the echoes that 'inhabit the garden'.

They are echoes because they are ghosts.

A ghost is, as it were, the echo a human being leaves behind after death. That is why these echoes are said to *inhabit* the garden. The problem with this exegesis is that we are forced to specify the vulgar, tainted word—'ghosts'—which Eliot so continently refuses to use even once. Instead, he gives us a potent periphrasis—*echoes*. As in 'Marina', as in 'Mr. Apollinax', Eliot shows himself a genius of deflection. In 'Marina', Eliot rethought the deadly sins. Here he remakes the whole ghost story topos with a single sustained act of restraint. Kipling's great ghost story '"They"' is clearly a source for Eliot's children, laughing and hidden among the leaves—and Kipling's story itself broke new ground by seeing ghosts, not as terrifying, but as consoling and heart-breaking. Henry James's 'The Turn of the Screw' may be another influence. James, in his preface, drew attention to his own restraint. He didn't supply the specifics of the children's corruption by Quint and Miss Jessel. In fact, it could only be one thing—sexual abuse— which he would have found it impossible to specify, given the Victorian moral climate. So his continence wasn't quite the literary act of conscious choice he presented it as.

Here, Eliot's ghosts are far from their clichéd literary models: the context is childhood memory ('our first world') and the ghosts are parental, surely: 'There they were, dignified, invisible, / Moving without pressure, over the dead leaves.' The adjective of genius here is 'dignified'—so unexpected, so plausible, so *real*. Only Nabokov has been so capable of patiently imagining how ghosts might actually *be*.[2] But you have to believe in them—as Nabokov did—to make the necessary effort. I have used the word 'genius' twice, in this and the previous paragraph. I mean it both times.

Eliot adds to his ghosts a moment of enlightenment: 'the surface glittered out of heart of light.' This is a brilliantly managed negotiation between the authentically mystical and the optical illusion: between 'the lotus', the Buddhist symbol of enlightenment, and Eliot's insistence on the drably familiar, the 'brown edged' concrete transformed by sunlight, 'filled with water out of sunlight'.

This management of the mystical is something from which Seamus Heaney has clearly learned, as *Station Island* (1984) shows. There 'le spectre en plein jour'—its ghostly entrances and exits—is smoothly managed thanks to Eliot's example of how to fuse the extraordinary with the quotidian: 'when something came to life in the driving mirror'; 'he trembled like a heatwave and faded'. And this apparition sidling into existence clearly apes the self-cancelling, mesmeric, indirect syntax of *Burnt Norton*: 'I had come to the edge of the water, / soothed by just looking, idling over it / as if it were a clear barometer // or a mirror, when his reflection / did not appear but I sensed a presence / entering into my concentration // on not being concentrated as he spoke / my name.' In *Omeros* (chapter XII), you can see Derek Walcott's botched, fatally indebted copy of Eliot when he describes his encounter with his father Warwick's ghost: Eliot's drained pool full of mystical water becomes a defunct fountain where, 'it seemed', 'water sprang in plumes'.

The obvious mistake for Eliot to make in the subsequent quartets would be to replicate the strategy of *Burnt Norton*—in which syntax opposes momentum to cancellation. In *East Coker*, Eliot's revenants again subvert the ghost story topos, but in a radically different way. They are almost paradoxical in their earthiness. They aren't spectral but literally clodhopping—chthonic aboriginals, Bruegel peasants 'Lifting heavy feet in clumsy shoes'. With their convincing introduction Eliot extends and diversifies his methods in *Burnt Norton*. As formerly, the opening insists on the prosaic—'a factory, or a by-pass'[3]—but shifts the tone from the bureaucratic to the biblical, to the antitheses of *Ecclesiastes*: 'Old stone to new building.' The last line of the first paragraph refers to the motto of Mary, Queen of Scots: 'And to shake the tattered arras woven with a silent motto.' That motto is '*En ma fin est mon commencement*', 'In my end is my beginning'—which is here reversed. The mention of the 'silent motto' brings the paragraph full circle, but closure also allows Eliot to begin his second paragraph with a natural reprise of the first line: 'In my beginning is my end.'

Eliot's subject is now the walk towards the village of East Coker—leaving behind those arterial roads for 'the deep lane / Shuttered with branches'. It is recognisable and ordinary, but spiked with muted oddnesses. 'Where you lean against a bank while a van passes' is an experience known to anyone who has been to Devon or Cornwall. But 'dark in the afternoon', as well as being realistic, is tinged with the idea of darkness at noon—eclipse at the crucifixion and the rending of the temple veil. The idea that 'the deep lane insists on the direction' is both banal and reminiscent of 'The Love Song of J. Alfred Prufrock': 'Streets that follow like a tedious argument / Of insidious intent / To lead you to an overwhelming question . . . '. We register, too, the inversion and blunt caesura of 'in the electric heat / Hypnotised'. Its strangeness, though, is countered by the pseudoscientific distinction in the immediately subsequent line about the nature of the light, 'absorbed, not refracted, by grey stone'. It is difficult to see how stone *could* refract light. But the scientific distinction is reassuring in its tone.

So reassuring, in fact, that readers do not notice that their surrogate journey has been circular. It began with light falling 'Across the open field', proceeds to the village and its dahlias, and reaches 'that open field'—where the peasant ghosts are maladroitly cavorting. Eliot's lines are, then, a perfect illustration of the motto, 'In my beginning is my end'. Not the flat, overridden contradictions of *Burnt Norton,* then, but something more gradualist, making its effects subliminally, until we reach an impossible endpoint like an Escher drawing.

The actual description of the dead peasants ('long since under earth') is inaugurated with a repeated muted imperative: 'If you do not come too close, if you do not come too close.' (The doubled 'if' is tripled in *Little Gidding* in a deliberate repetition of the repetition: 'If you came this way', 'If you came at night like a broken king, / If you came by day not knowing what you came for'.) This repetition is a rhetorical marker, but Eliot's main device is the *ostranenie*[4] produced by the orthography taken from *The Boke of the Governour* by Eliot's ancestor Sir Thomas Elyot. It is surprising how much mileage can be generated from so little fuel—though not to anyone who has registered that Caliban's idiolect in Browning's 'Caliban upon Setebos' is largely created by two simple effects. Browning suppresses the definite and indefinite articles and has Caliban refer to himself in the third person. Eliot's means are even more laconic: 'In daunsinge, signifying matrimonie.'[5] The spelling of 'dancing' implies a variant pronunciation, but 'matrimonie' is an effect for the eye only, as are 'eche', 'concorde', 'necessarye' and 'whiche'. But 'eche' one does an enormous amount of work, a surprising amount of work in the field of defamiliarisation. When he was writing the cockney pub scene in *The Waste Land*, Eliot noted in the margin of his draft: 'I want to avoid trying to show pronunciation by spelling.' He knew, then, how powerful spelling could be as a literary effect—and that restraint was therefore necessary if the effect was not to be overdone. In *East Coker* he gets it just right—five lines out of twenty-four. In *The Rock* he gets it wrong. Or the Reverend Howson, credited with the cockney dialogue in Eliot's preface, gets it wrong.

Did Eliot believe in ghosts? Had they any real place in his doctrinal beliefs? Or were they merely a reworking of a useful literary topos? Eliot occasionally drops hints of unusual, unorthodox beliefs.

Like rebirth.

At the end of his Dante essay, for example, he discusses the *Vita Nuova* as 'a sequence of beautiful poems connected by a curious vision-literature prose'.

As well as being 'vision-literature', the *Vita Nuova* is, Eliot argues, 'anti-romantic' and realist. To understand this fusion, we have to make an effort of historical imagination: 'to pass through the looking-glass into a world which is just as reasonable as our own'. To do this, says Eliot, is 'as difficult and hard as re-birth'. Rebirth might simply be an analogy, an index of the extent of the change required. But the word 'hard' makes it sound like something Eliot might have experienced. Had he written—as he easily could have done—that it was difficult and hard as *birth*, there would be no strangeness. The mystical experience that opens *Burnt Norton* seems authentic and credible to me. It has literary sources also, but, they serve a real experience rather than create it. The subsequent ghosts in *East Coker* and *Little Gidding* are, I think, brilliantly contrived variants, rather than actual experiences. On the other hand, Eliot, worrying over *Little Gidding*, proposed to John Hayward the introduction of 'some acute personal reminiscence (never to be explicated, of course, but to give power from well below the surface)'.

The ghosts of *Burnt Norton* owe something to Kipling's ' "They" '. The atavistic peasantry of *East Coker* owes something to Kipling's 'The Way through the Woods'—a poem Eliot singled out, in his introduction to *A Choice of Kipling's Verse*, as a 'remarkable innovation'. Kipling's second stanza begins with the conditional Eliot employs so tellingly: 'Yet, if you enter the woods / Of a summer evening late . . . '. What follows on this condition is a sighting of ghosts and the Eliotean note of contradiction: 'You will hear the beat of a horse's feet, / And the swish of a skirt in the dew, / Steadily cantering through / The misty solitudes, / As though they perfectly knew / The old lost road through the woods . . . / But there is no road through the woods.'

Kipling is there, too, at the beginning of *The Dry Salvages*, which alludes to his story 'The Bridge Builders': 'Then only a problem confronting the builder of bridges.' In the Kipling story, which is also a source for Golding's *The Spire*, the engineer Findlayson is carried away as the Ganges, a 'strong brown god', floods and threatens to sweep away his bridge. He fetches up on an island, where he hallucinates all the gods in the Hindu pantheon— thanks to opium he has borrowed from Peroo, his Indian foreman, to fight off exhaustion. Kipling's story outlines a theme familiar from *The Waste Land*: that the gods are remade constantly and put to service in different religions: 'they [human beings] will do no more than change the names, and that we have seen a thousand times.' Small wonder that Eliot should move comfortably from Krishna to the Virgin Mary. The other theme of 'The Bridge Builders' is the eventual demise of the gods altogether—the sense that man no longer needs religion. This in a story where the river is a strong brown god full of dead bodies and where this phrase occurs: 'The end shall be as it was in the beginning', meaning godless.

There are no ghosts in *The Dry Salvages*. In *Little Gidding*, though, Eliot again gives us a variant on the ghost topos. Rather than choosing from the many unusual ghosts available—self-haunting ghosts, for example, or Tokens, which are wraiths of the living—Eliot *invents* 'a familiar compound ghost'. By 'compound' he means, perhaps, more than one dead person, but certainly something that coexists with normal surface reality—something simultaneously flesh and blood and unknown. He is, I think, consciously or unconsciously, playing on the word 'familiar' as an adjective and as a noun. As a noun, two of its meanings apply here: 'one well or long acquainted' and 'a spirit or demon supposed to attend a person at call'. Two strangers meet. They are also intimate. 'The eyes of a familiar compound ghost / Both intimate and unidentifiable.'

Unlike the procedure used in previous quartets, here Eliot's method is not gradualist, a series of linguistic triggers, each of which accelerates the reader to the impossible, the mystical. Initially, we are plunged into paradox: 'the ending of *interminable night*' [my italics]. The air raid and the enemy bomber are presented not prosaically but euphuistically in lines verging on the affected: 'After the dark dove with the flickering tongue / Had passed below the horizon of his homing.' Thereafter, reversing his usual method, Eliot's manner clarifies into the simply expository, but for one inversion ('the urban dawn wind unresisting') and one last paradox— 'I met one walking, loitering and hurried'—whose function is to remind us gently that things aren't exactly normal.

For the rest, despite the evident weirdness, Eliot's tone couldn't be clearer or more straightforward. The model for Eliot's pastiche is Dante's *Inferno* canto XV, where Dante recognises the face of his poetic master, Ser Brunetto Latini. At first, Dante thinks he is looking at one of the anonymous damned, with a face like someone out of Beckett—'*lo cotto aspetto*', roasted features. But gradually he makes out the familiar face. Compare the flamboyant euphuism of the start with the clarity of Eliot sifting the complications: 'I caught the sudden look of some dead master / Whom I had known, forgotten, half-recalled / Both one and many'; 'I was still the same, / Knowing myself yet being someone other.'

By comparison, the opening of *Little Gidding* has a managed, contrived feel. This may be because Eliot is reprising a passage spoken by the Tempter in *Murder in the Cathedral*: 'Spring has come in winter. Snow in the branches / Shall float as sweet as blossoms. Ice along the ditches / Mirror the sunlight.' He is also perhaps attempting to summon up and redress Pater's image of life's brevity in *The Renaissance*, 'this short day of frost and sun'. In *Little Gidding*, Eliot wants to create 'the spring time / But not in time's covenant'. We are offered a visual pun—the sight of snow as blossom on branches—and, bingo, spring and winter are conflated. The fusion is bolstered by some clever touches of pseudoparadox: 'The brief sun *flames* the ice' [my italics]; 'In windless cold that is the heart's heat', meaning the cold outside magnifies internal warmth. There is a suggestion of occluded transcendence in Eliot's reminiscence and brilliant refashioning of the biblical seeing 'through a glass darkly': 'reflecting in a watery mirror / A glare that is blindness in the early afternoon.' The medial caesurae mimic the temporal division that is to be cancelled—but the whole passage is more an emblem of time's simultaneity than an enactment of time's simultaneity. It is competent, as Eliot knows. And it admits its own contrivance, I think, when we read of a harder task altogether: 'Where is the summer, the unimaginable / Zero summer?' Eliot means a summer when the temperature is at freezing point. The question is rhetorical. The adjective 'unimaginable' is an admission of failure.

But the admission of failure is a deliberate theme of *Four Quartets*: 'That was a way of putting it—not very satisfactory: / A periphrastic study in a worn-out poetical fashion', Eliot comments in *East Coker*. What is 'it' here? 'It' is exactly what 'it' is at the start of *Little Gidding*—the simultaneity of time. That is, time not as something chronological and linear, with a past, present, and future, in that order—but time as an omnipresent in which these categories are collapsed. *The Waste Land* was predicated on this implicit *assumption*—an assumption Eliot in *Four Quartets* sets out to 'demonstrate' on several occasions, lyrically and otherwise. Thus the seasonal fudge of *East Coker* section II: 'What is the late November doing / With the disturbance of the spring / And creatures of the summer heat', culminating in 'Late roses filled with snow'.[6] More baffling is *Burnt Norton* section II, the notorious 'garlic and sapphires' passage, which is often explained away by categorising it as 'symboliste' poetry. Eliot's argument here is that nature is a fusion of the changing and the immutable—the organic garlic and the unchanging sapphire. The Earth's axis—around which this material is clotted—is also paradoxical, in that the geometric axis, the axiomatic axis, is still though everything turns around it. [A similar idea is that the line is only a point in motion.] Eliot figures sequential, conventional time as the boar hound pursuing the boar, the one behind, the other ahead. And Eliot tells us they are 'reconciled among the stars'—that is, no one chases, no one is pursued; there is simultaneity *sub specie aeternitatis*. The same idea lies behind the opaque lines: 'The trilling wire in the blood / Sings below inveterate scars / Appeasing long forgotten wars.' Here the poetry touches on race memory. In 'Rannoch, by Glencoe' (1935) the pass carries the faint memory of its martial past: 'The road winds in / Listlessness of ancient war.' In the *Burnt Norton* passage, Eliot is mooting the idea that, although the scars are old and healed and the wars that caused them long forgotten, the original excitement is there in our blood consciousness. We still prove it on our pulses: 'The trilling wire in the blood.'[7] The past, then, is never past. It inhabits the present. The unsatisfactoriness of this lyric evocation is implicit in Eliot's immediately subsequent, calculatedly prosaic gloss, in which the 'bedded axle-tree' becomes 'the still point of the turning world'.

Of course, the limitations of conventional lyric poetry had been central to Eliot's anti-'poetic' agenda from the beginning.[8] In *Four Quartets*, the distrust broadens to engross writing itself, usually in the reflective, discursive fifth and final sections that meditate on the difficulty of the task in hand. Take section V of *Burnt Norton*. If you want to demonstrate that 'all is always now', then you will find that 'Words strain, / Crack and sometimes break under the burden'. In section V of *East Coker*, 'one has only learnt to get the better of words / For the thing one no longer has to say'. In *East Coker*, Eliot also says, 'You say I am repeating / Something I have said before'. Indeed. The difficulty of expression, the crack and strain, was there in his essay on the metaphysical poets, and its injunction 'to dislocate if necessary, language into [his] meaning'.

It isn't an easy job—establishing the reality of a condition that will make the anomalous mystical moment at once impossible yet possible. In *Four Quartets*, there are several kinds of time, but the main ones are three. First, normal sequential time by which we all live; second, unalterable simultaneous time; third, mystical experience, which takes place outside all time but can only be remembered *in* time, what Eliot in *The Dry Salvages* section V calls 'The point of intersection of the timeless / With time'. Valerie Eliot reports that Eliot thought of adding an epigraph from *Pickwick Papers* to *Four Quartets*: 'What a rum thing time is, ain't it, Neddy?'

Parallel to the theme of the obsolescence of poetic mastery is the theme of old age—and the bleak realities of its unwisdom, absence of serenity, its impotent rage, its discontent, its disenchantment, its retrospective sense of shame. Often inaccurately compared to Yeats's monotone, monochrome 'frenzy', Eliot's portrait of old age is truer, less self-dramatising, more telling—detailed where Yeats is melodramatic.

The analogy between music and poetry is implicit in Eliot's overall title. Obviously, the string quartet is made up of movements, as Eliot's poems are, and there is different instrumentation, just as Eliot mixes the lyric ('Ash on an old man's sleeve') with the prosaic ('There is, it seems to us, / At best, only a limited value' ...). But I think Eliot is careful to avoid the predictability of strict patterning. The *sensation* of repetition is vivid in readers of *Four Quartets* but nothing is mechanically repeated. The analogy I would make is with Kundera's *The Book of Laughter and Forgetting*, a novel by a writer with a proper musical education, the son of a professional pianist and musicologist. Kundera tells his reader what the form of his novel is: 'This entire book is a novel in the form of variations.' Likewise, Eliot's title is frank: *Four Quartets.* Kundera, though, knows how musical variations work. He continues: 'the individual parts follow each other like individual stretches of a journey leading towards a theme, a thought, a single situation, *the sense of which fades in the distance*.' [my italics] Ultimately, the organisation of *Four Quartets* eludes us, too. For example, the meditations on writing usually occur in the fifth section of each quartet. In *Little Gidding*, it is in section II that we read 'For last year's words belong to last year's language / And next year's words await another voice'.

It is true that similar literary reflections are to be found in *Little Gidding* section V, but they are attenuated and mechanical—there because they have to be there and not much better than the advice you might expect in a superior creative writing class. Or, ironically enough, Arnold's preface to his *Poems* (1853) and its exhortation to prize *Architectonicè*, the whole over the particular effect, and to 'subordinate[s] expression to that which it is designed to express': 'where every word is at home, / Taking its place to support the others, / The word neither diffident nor ostentatious.'

Section II of *Little Gidding* fulfils its lyric quota, too. It begins compellingly with a reminiscence of *Burnt Norton*: 'Ash on an old man's sleeve / Is all the ash burnt roses leave.' The remainder of the lyric over-systematically sets out to cover the four elements and falls foul of its couplets. 'Water and fire shall rot / The marred foundations we forgot': *fire* shall *rot*? And what does this mean?: 'The parched eviscerate soil / Gapes at the vanity of toil, / Laughs without mirth.' Evidently we are confronted with the wasteland, the dust bowl, the 'eviscerate soil' created by misguided farming methods. But how can *soil* 'laugh[s] without mirth'? Maybe cracks in the parched ground are mouth-like and can therefore 'gape' and 'laugh'.

The line anticipates the more intelligible later lines, 'the laceration / Of laughter at what ceases to amuse'—one of the ironic 'gifts' of old age. Are we then to assume in the lyric a conflation of old man and destroyed place? Just as, in 'Marina', the aged body of Pericles is figured in the ramshackle boat, 'the rigging weak and the canvas rotten'? If so, the recapitulation of destruction in all four quartets would also be a version of bodily decrepitude. And the 'sanctuary and choir' of the chapel at Little Gidding will be ruined in time like the individual body—destroyed by 'Time the destroyer'.

The attenuations of sense in the lyrics (sections II and IV) are a difficulty throughout *Four Quartets*—most obviously in the second section of *The Dry Salvages*, where, in a simplified version of the sestina, the six rhyme words occur five times each ('wailing', 'trailing', 'failing', 'sailing', 'bailing') with the last stanza ('wailing') repeating the first with one significant difference. The 'unprayable' becomes the 'barely prayable'—optimism of sorts. These impacted lyric interludes and the passages of prosaic exposition sometimes seem written to a theory of the long poem—as requiring a variety of methods, many of them 'unpoetical' and functional. Obviously, this is of a piece with the early poetry's triumphant use of the unpoetical—the *Boston Evening Transcript*. But one recalls, too, Coleridge chiding Wordsworth for writing *Lyrical Ballads* against his natural bent: 'Will he [the reader] not decide that the one [quotation] was written because the poet *would* so write, and the other because he could not entirely repress the force and grandeur of his mind?'

Undeniably, *Four Quartets* has its faults—for instance, the elementary tautology of 'anxious worried women' in section I of *The Dry Salvages*. But the passages documenting in undeniable detail 'the moment in and out of time' are the most successful attempts at the mystical in poetry since Wordsworth's spots of time in *The Prelude*—themselves a refiguration of the mystical.

And these mystical passages relate closely to the figure in Eliot's carpet. They are the moments when, fleetingly, the poet touches on the buried life of his spirit. 'Human kind / Cannot bear very much reality'—but occasionally, Eliot shows us by example, humankind manages to breakthrough into this occluded spiritual reality. There are in *Four Quartets* other kinds of buried life—the 'strong brown god' of the river 'present in the nursery bedroom', for example. Or Eliot's explicit assertion in *The Dry Salvages* section II that 'the past experience revived in the meaning / Is not the experience of one life only / But of many generations'. Compare *Little Gidding*: 'We are born with the dead: / See, they return, and bring us with them.'

You wouldn't expect such a fundamental intuition not to inform Eliot's ambitious last poem. And, of course, the buried life fuels the drama, too.

Five

THE DRAMA

SWEENEY AGONISTES (published in *The Criterion*, October 1926 and January 1927) is a dramatic fragment, half Greek choral, half Jazz riff—Aeschylus on sax—powerful, lowlife, poetic noir, flirting with menace, melodramatic, centred on the desire to 'do a girl in'. It owes something to the 'Circe' episode in *Ulysses*, where inanimate objects are characters with lines. Here the telephone goes 'Ting a ling ling'. *Sweeney Agonistes* also looks forward to the jovial menace of Harold Pinter—the notorious weasel under the cocktail cabinet, an image Pinter once used to describe his work (only to repudiate it later).

Eliot's first full dramatic work is *The Rock* (1934), a pageant play written to raise money for forty-five churches in the northern suburbs of London. Eliot feared that his 'meagre poetic gifts' were exhausted and the pageant play provided the stimulus of a commission. Jointly authored with E Martin Browne, it was a popular success but alienated many of Eliot's former admirers who found it poetically tepid. In 1935, the brilliantly titled *Murder in the Cathedral*, about the martyrdom of St. Thomas à Becket, was performed in Canterbury Cathedral. In 1939, *The Family Reunion* opened at the Westminster Theatre. An interregnum followed in which Eliot wrote *Four Quartets*. Then, in 1948, he wrote *The Cocktail Party*. *The Confidential Clerk* followed in 1953. In 1958, *The Elder Statesman* opened at the Edinburgh Festival. Eliot's immense literary prestige meant that the plays were attentively and respectfully received. They are now of interest largely because they show Eliot addressing the problem of contemporary poetic drama and how it might be successfully achieved. The plays are also read as covert autobiography, alluding to Eliot's unhappy marriage—as they do, though not perhaps so literally as hostile critics like to think. As Eliot neared the end of his life, his themes become clearer—to us, and to him. So the plays address Eliot's lifelong preoccupation with discovering what we *really* feel under the carapace of convention. They attempt to access the buried lives of their protagonists. None of the plays is as genuinely dramatic as *The Waste Land*.

In 1951, Eliot lectured at Harvard on 'Poetry and Drama'. By then he had written everything he was to write for the stage except *The Confidential Clerk* and *The Elder Statesman*. When Shakespeare writes poetically rather than plainly, functionally, Eliot believes that he is writing 'for a moment beyond character'. And this proves to be exactly what Eliot believes poetic drama can do more naturally than prose drama, even when the prose drama is by Ibsen and Chekhov. 'Beyond character': this seems to mean that Shakespeare has unobtrusively grafted his own linguistic gift on to his character. But Eliot means something more than enrichment, verbal steroids, a surreptitious transfer of assets. He means this:

it seems to me that beyond the nameable, classifiable emotions and motives of our conscious life when directed towards action— the part of life which prose drama is wholly adequate to express— there is a fringe of indefinite extent, of feeling which we can only detect, so to speak, out of the corner of the eye and can never completely focus; of feeling of which we are only aware in a kind of temporary detachment from action.

Here poetic drama comes into its own: 'this peculiar range of sensibility can be expressed by dramatic poetry, at its moments of greatest intensity. At such moments, we touch the border of those feelings which only music can express.'[1]

In other words, the buried life.

In *Murder in the Cathedral*, for example, there is the discrepancy between the youthful, worldly Becket and the spiritually fastidious archbishop, whose consent to martyrdom is mystical: 'It is out of time that my decision is taken / If you call that decision / To which my whole being gives entire consent.' The Fourth Tempter voices the temptation buried so deep inside Becket that he is initially unprepared, surprised, to discover that spiritual pride is a factor in his willingness to embrace martyrdom.

The Family Reunion is an Agatha Christie country house whodunnit, crossed with darker forces—did Harry push his wife overboard, or was it wishful thinking, thinking driven by his dead (and buried) father's ancient desire to kill his wife? When Police Sergeant Winchell appears, the audience, like Harry, initially believes he has come to make an arrest; he has, however, come to report a road accident involving Harry's brother, John. A whodunnit, then, but one ghosted by Aeschylus's Orestes and the pursuing Furies. This potent exhumation is underlined by

Winchell's pointed, repeated mistake of thinking the birthday celebrations are for Harry and not for his mother: 'Good evening, my Lord. Good evening, Doctor. / Many happy . . . Oh, I'm sorry, my Lord, / I was thinking it was your birthday, not her Ladyship's.' Why the mistake? Because birthdays summon the phrase 'many happy *returns*'—a phrase echoed in Arthur's telegram—and we are about to witness, along with Agatha, Mary, and Downing (Harry's man) the return of the Furies, whose effect proves to be curiously benign. Harry: 'I must follow the bright angels.' This view of the Furies, usually seen as an avenging force, is supported by Downing: 'There's no harm in *them*, / I'll take my oath.'

On the contrary, there seems to be virtue in them. Eliot evidently sees Harry as a man seeking refuge from his fate, as a man in flight from his actions and thoughts. At Wishwood, for the first time, he sees the Furies from whom he has been in flight. And he feels better. The process here is analogous to abreaction in psychoanalysis. Though Eliot would probably reject any *intended* parallel, the alleviation of Harry's condition is not unlike a neurosis that is cured by identifying the site of trauma. In Harry's case, the curse is inherited from the marriage of his parents—a marriage so unhappy that Agatha had to persuade Harry's father not to murder Amy, who was pregnant with Harry.

It would be wrong to think of Aeschylus as merely a convenient narrative blueprint, bled of real meaning for Eliot. The thing about Matthew Arnold that most irritated Eliot was Arnold's contention that religion could be replaced by poetry. This depends on a fatally impoverished view of religion as a guide to morality and conduct. No wonder Eliot quotes Bradley on Arnold with so much relish:

Most of us, certainly the public which Mr. Arnold addresses, want something they can worship; and they will not find that in an hypostasised copy-book heading, which is not much more adorable than 'Honesty is the best policy', or 'Handsome is that handsome does', or various other edifying maxims, which have not yet come to an apotheosis.

Eliot was a man who believed in religious experience—in larger forces, in mystical experience, in the suprarational. In his essay on Pascal, he writes with the casual authority of firsthand experience: 'what can only be called mystical experience happens to many men who do not become mystics.' The birthday cake, the birthday candles, appear at the play's end. The ceremony of blowing out the candles is invested with the force of religious ritual—celebrating not birth but the final fulfilment of death and the end of a curse. It is as if this stale, familiar rigmarole has trace elements of something more religiously significant that has been buried under long custom.

In *The Cocktail Party*, the template is taken from Euripides's 'resurrection' play *Alcestis*—and the buried life is clear when the cocktails mimic ancient libations at the end of act 2. But, in any case, Edward is a man whose true personality is occluded by a social self: as he explains to his wife Lavinia, 'You're still trying to invent a personality for me / Which will only keep me away from myself'. Before Lavinia's entrance (when she has left Edward), the Unidentified Guest, Sir Henry Harcourt-Reilly is less a character than Eliot's mouthpiece:

Edward: To what does this lead?
Unidentified Guest: To finding out

What you really are. What you really feel.
What you really are among other people.
Most of the time we take ourselves for granted,
As we have to, and live on a little knowledge
About ourselves as we were. Who are you now?
You don't know any more than I do.

In *The Confidential Clerk*, when Colby Simpkins's true parentage is revealed, he is able to emulate his real father as an organist. Thus, true to his buried life, Simpkins loses the awkward intuitive feeling of being miscast as confidential clerk to Sir Claude Mulhammer, who thinks, incorrectly, that Simpkins is his son. Lord Claverton in *The Elder Statesman* is dogged by a life of lies— his corruption of Culverwell, his jilting of Maisie Mountjoy—as Eliot's theme of inner unknowability declines into the more easily comprehensible, less interesting subset of hypocrisy. His ne'er-do-well son, Michael Claverton-Ferry, continues the idea of biological inheritance from *The Confidential Clerk* and the idea of the family curse from *The Family Reunion*.

Eliot's belief that the childrens' teeth are set on edge by the sour grapes eaten by their fathers—that the lives of the parents are buried alive in their children—is a theme he touched on in *The Dry Salvages*: 'I have said before / That the past experience revived in the meaning / Is not the experience of one life only / But of many generations.' And *The Rock* (1934), Eliot's pageant play, is predicated on the same idea. The builders in *The Rock* are contemporary cockneys and Anglo-Saxon ancestors—a hybrid fusion mirrored in their names, Fred/Alfred, Bert/Ethelbert. Recurrence is one more version of the buried life.

The buried life usually identified by critics in *The Family Reunion* (1939) is that of Eliot's first wife. Carole Seymour-Jones's execrable biography of Vivien Haigh-Wood took its title, *Painted Shadow*, from Eliot's play. There, Harry, Lord Monchensey, the heir to Wishwood, may have pushed his difficult wife overboard. Or not. Is the wish to be taken for the deed? Eliot leaves it ambiguous. Certainly, the desire is there, if not the actual deed. The crucial ambiguity has, of course, been coarsened into a kind of certainty—that Eliot 'murdered' his first wife. There is no doubt that Vivien Eliot was a difficult woman, who would have tried anyone's patience. Nor is there any doubt that Eliot experienced profound guilt after his divorce. Equally, Eliot's marriage was not an unmitigated disaster. As well as infidelity (on Vivien's part, with Bertrand Russell), there was tenderness and happiness which have been written out of the record in the interest of febrile narrative. After the separation, Eliot was protective. He avoided confrontation but displayed 'consistent concern'—my wife, Ann Pasternak Slater's phrase, taken from her demolition of the Seymour-Jones's biography in *Areté* (Winter 2001), a review essay that is also the best account of Eliot's marriage to be found anywhere.

Nevertheless, Eliot's difficult relationship with Vivien clearly feeds *The Family Reunion,* and it is an act of exemplary artistic courage. Although Pasternak Slater demonstrates Eliot's concern, and shows it to be sincere in private as well as in public, his play discloses what Eliot was so careful to repress in his daily life. There is a crucial distinction to be made here—repress, not *suppress.* And the distinction was one of which Eliot was acutely conscious: in *The Family Reunion*, Harry's servant, Downing, volunteers this analysis of his employer, 'I always said his Lordship / Suffered from what they call a kind of repression'.

And what did Eliot repress? The desire to be rid of his wife—definitively, permanently, impossibly. Short of murder, a clean break was impossible in actuality, where complications claimed Eliot until Vivien's death in 1947. The artist, then, differs from the man, by acknowledging his buried life—what he *really* feels.

Agatha, Harry's aunt, is the character who most *obviously* embodies the theme of the buried life: 'What people know me as, / The efficient principal of a women's college— / That is the surface. There is a deeper / Organisation, which your question disturbs.' Now and then, the hidden self takes over from the social self—and proves to have a weakness for a more poetic register, to be gifted with a greater stylistic reach. As the characters succumb to these dark psychic imperatives, they are reminiscent of the prince in *The Princess*—whose catalepsy is the pretext for Tennyson's lyricism, for that moment with the mandolin, that flourish at the theatre organ. After their poetic riffs, the characters come round, unburdened, a touch glazed and laconic. Agatha (part 2, scene 2): 'What have I been saying? I think I was saying . . . ' Harry (part 1, scene 2): 'What have we been saying? I think I was saying . . . '

Eliot's challenge as a dramatist is to negotiate his two registers—the prosaic and the poetic—registers that reflect his overall theme of the gap between the individual's real personality and the social construct. This theme means that Eliot always requires a stylistic contrast and cannot merge the two registers. There has to be a pronounced demarcation.

However, it is also true that though poetic drama by definition requires poetry, the poetry has to be naturalised in some way, if it is not to seem artificial at best, or arch at its worst. In 1951, in 'Poetry and Drama', Eliot makes it clear that the great ambition is transparency, so the audience attends to the meaning of the poetry, not to the poetry. As the plays go on, it is true to say that Eliot becomes less poetic, more and more prosy and humorous. In the same 1951 lecture, he ruefully acknowledges that, by purging his dramatic verse in his third play, *The Cocktail Party*, he may have gone too far: 'it is perhaps an open question whether there is any poetry in the play at all.'

In *Murder in the Cathedral*, this dilemma is at its least pressing. The cathedral setting and historical subject matter make a heightened linguistic idiom acceptable and natural. When the chorus recites, 'The New Year waits, breathes, waits, whispers in darkness', the audience experiences no aesthetic discomfort, but only gratitude for the brilliant verb 'breathes'. When the Second Priest summarises the instability of competing forces, we wobble mentally between Eliot's perfectly competing genitives: 'the perpetual wash of tides of balance of forces of barons and landholders'. The difficulty for Eliot in *Murder in the Cathedral* is the sense of comfortable anachronism, of facile pastiche, undermining his modernist credentials. In Picasso or Stravinsky's classical periods the classical isn't pure. It is self-conscious and includes an ironic dimension. Picasso's line is clean, thin, representational, then momentarily given to unpredictable laxities, detours that will enlarge one limb without disrupting the mood. Stravinsky's trombones will suddenly introduce a raspberry of vulgarity and gusto into the *Pulcinella* suite.

Eliot's solution to the need to signal his modernity is more radical—and recycled from *The Waste Land*'s 'A Game of Chess', where the coarse cockney colloquialism overlays the baroque syntax of the previous passage. In *Murder*, as the knights seek to justify their action, Eliot gives us the authentic modern corporate voice of conference-speak: 'No one regrets the necessity for violence more than we do'; 'Morville has given us a great deal to think about'; 'the Archbishop *had* to be put out of the way—and personally I had a tremendous admiration for him ...'.

In the other plays, unfortunately, Eliot has no convention to assist him—a convention like that of the musical, say, in which normal dialogue suddenly gives way to song. The characters can sound simply stilted like end-stopped, one-sentence refugees from Virgina Woolf's *The Waves*:

> Ivy: I do not trust Charles with his confident vulgarity, acquired from worldly associates.
>
> Gerald: Ivy is only concerned for herself, and her credit among her shabby genteel acquaintance.
>
> Violet: Gerald is certain to make some blunder, he is useless out of the army.
>
> Charles: Violet is afraid that her status as Amy's sister will be diminished.

Not *dialogue*, then, but serial monologue.

Taking his image from a description in *Brideshead Revisited*, John Carey once wrote that Eliot's plays were like an enormous clanking Victorian water heater that produces vast quantities of steam and noise but only a trickle of tepid water. Clearly the plot of *The Confidential Clerk* strains credulity—however much one invokes the world of Shakespeare's late romances and Eliot's comic intention. *The Family Reunion* never succeeds in marrying Greek tragedy and the genre Auden called 'The Guilty Vicarage'. The melodramatic plot of *The Elder Statesman* might have been concocted by Oscar Wilde at his weakest, the Wilde of *An Ideal Husband*.

But the real problem is that the plays are acts of exposition, not of embodiment.[2] They are useful to us readers, of course, because they provide so much coherent recapitulation. As drama, they fail in varying degrees, because we couldn't care less what, say, Edward Chamberlayne *really* feels. Edward isn't a character. He is an illustration—almost a slide. The buried life is a theorem for Eliot by now, an over-familiar, zestless platitude, which in *The Elder Statesman* has dwindled to a clutch of guilty secrets— hypocrisy, its final, depleted incarnation. In the early poetry, the idea is animated by all of Eliot's young man's savagery, all his militant hatred of sentimentality, all his aggressive insistence on what we really feel—how unpleasant that can be, and frequently how meagre.

Six

THE CRITICISM

IN HIS LECTURE ON MATTHEW ARNOLD in *The Use of Poetry and the Use of Criticism* (1933), Eliot remarked that 'the majority of critics can be expected only to parrot the opinions of the last master of criticism . . . until a new authority comes to introduce some order'. Eliot was a new critical master. When Vladimir Nabokov applied for a teaching post in the comparative literature department at Harvard, he didn't get the job. Roman Jakobson complained that Nabokov's critical judgements were eccentric. Harry Levin countered that Nabokov was a very distinguished novelist. Jakobson's quip carried the day: 'You wouldn't employ an elephant to run the Zoology department.' In Eliot's case, though, his status as a poet gave authority to his criticism. His difficult poetry was taken seriously—by everyone except Nabokov, who thought it fraudulent—it was lent authority by the sound judgements in Eliot's criticism and its dazzling range of reference. The poetry and the criticism were a great double act.

Eliot was an assiduous and indefatigable reviewer and essayist. His articles and lectures were reissued and preserved in a steady stream of books: *The Sacred Wood* (1920); *For Lancelot Andrewes* (1928); *Selected Essays* (1932); the Charles Eliot Norton lectures at Harvard as *The Use of Poetry and the Use of Criticism* (1933); the Page-Barbour lectures at the University of Virginia as *After Strange Gods* (1934); three lectures at Corpus Christi College, Cambridge, as *The Idea of a Christian Society* (1939); *Notes towards the Definition of Culture* (1948); *On Poetry and Poets* (1957); and the posthumous *To Criticise the Critic* (1965). In 1953, Penguin Books published Eliot's *Selected Prose*, edited by John Hayward, in a printing of forty thousand copies. An appropriate tribute to a man whose critical writings had set the agenda for the best part of the twentieth century.

One reason Eliot is a remarkable literary critic is his theoretical inclination and, above all, his instinct for definition. As a trained philosopher, he brings to literary criticism an habitual analytical bent, which he was later to mock as his 'reputation for affecting pedantic precision'. In 'American Language and Literature' (1953), he proposes to analyse what is meant by 'the American language'. But he specifically, wryly, humorously refrains from asking, 'What is literature?' Yet the question 'What is "rhetoric"?' is at the heart of ' "Rhetoric" and Poetic Drama' (1919). Eliot was unafraid of the unflinching forensic approach to what Stephen Dedalus calls 'those big words that make us so unhappy'. He had a philosopher's unfazed tidy mind—a fondness for discriminations and microdistinctions. But while he was sorting things into their proper pigeonholes, Eliot was also capable of thinking out of the box altogether. He was a very bold conceptualist. The downsizing accountant will suddenly morph into the intellectual astronaut making for outer space. It is a heady hybridity.

In an uncollected essay, 'Experiment in Criticism' (1929), he begins by distinguishing between 'traditional' criticism and 'experimental' criticism—characteristically pointing out that the 'traditional' may be 'experimental' if the critic reverts to 'masters who have been forgotten'. Eliot's analytical distinctions are subtle, clear, frequently counterintuitive, and given to proper complication. 'I want to distinguish between the particular and general functions [of poetry]', he writes in 'The Social Function of Poetry', 'so that we shall know what we are not talking about'. And Eliot proceeds to analyse the particular functions of specific types of poetry—distinguishing, for example, didactic poetry from satiric poetry, though they have an instructive function in common. In passing, he points to an overlap between satire and burlesque, because both seek to induce mirth. He notes that dramatic poetry can make a collective impression in the theatre. He touches on philosophical poetry. And he concludes that the *function* of all these different types could as easily be carried out by prose.

Only then does he address the task he has set himself, which is to show that the function of poetry *of all types* is to keep our language alive—'first to preserve, and second to extend and improve'. This is important, Eliot asserts, because our ability to feel depends on it. This is typical—exciting and unprovable, a plangent proposition whose dubiety is masked by Eliot's analytic precision elsewhere in the essay.

To this analytic ability one must add wide reading (in ' "Rhetoric" and Poetic Drama' (1919) Eliot refers casually to the Renaissance prose writers John Lyly, Roger Ascham, and Sir Thomas

Elyot), a fine grasp of detail, a gift for apt quotation, and a confident, persuasive, strikingly individual radical taste. Here is a critic capable of seeing that Edward Lear's 'The Yongy-Bongy Bo' and 'The Dong with the Luminous Nose' are 'poems of unrequited love—"blues" in fact'. He is capable, too, of describing Milton's diction as 'a perpetual sequence of original acts of lawlessness'. And of describing Milton as 'the greatest master of free verse in our language'. Both verdicts are meant as praise. Only a critical genius would compare *Paradise Lost* and *Finnegans Wake* as fields of exclusive aural experimentation.

Greatly gifted, then—but not infallible. Eliot could be spectacularly wrong. You wonder at his unwavering support for the unreadable Wyndham Lewis when, in *The Dial* (April 1922), he dismissed Frost: 'his verse, it is regretfully said, is uninteresting, and what is uninteresting is unreadable, and what is unreadable is not read. There, that is done.' This is eccentric, of course, but also surprising because Eliot's poetry and Frost's had something in common—the desire to divest poetry of rhetoric, in favour of something more nearly conversational. Eliot is candid about this shared modernist programme in 'Milton II' (1947): 'But Milton does, as I have said, represent poetry at the extreme limit from prose; and it was one of our tenets that verse should have the virtues of prose, that diction should become assimilated to cultivated contemporary speech, before aspiring to the elevation of poetry.'

Nor is Eliot correct to upbraid Arnold for his limited scholarship. A glance at Arnold's *Essays in Criticism* (1865) will acquit him. Homer, Heine, Sophocles, Spinoza, Voltaire, Tolstoy, the de Guérins, Joubert, La Bruyère, Renan, Sainte-Beuve, Marcus Aurelius, Goethe, and all the English poets. Eliot is also wrong, in *After Strange Gods*, to deny D. H. Lawrence a sense of humour and allege an 'incapacity for what we ordinarily call thinking'. Lawrence mistrusted the rational, but on perfectly reasoned grounds. Mistrust is not incapacity. Eliot's are widely shared prejudices, but the charges cannot survive beside Lawrence's analyses of Hardy's novels—or the great comic quarrels in *Women in Love*, Anna's giggles in *The Rainbow*, or the detached dog observing through its paws Mellors and Connie making love.

A similar prejudice underlies the assertion, in *The Use of Poetry*, that Wordsworth's 'inspiration never having been of that sudden, fitful and terrifying kind that visited Coleridge, he was never, apparently, troubled by the consciousness of having lost it'. Loss is the very subject of 'Tintern Abbey' and 'Ode: Intimations of Immortality', as well as much of *The Prelude*.

It is unusual for Eliot to misread poetry, but there is a rare example in 'Milton I', in which he takes a speech by Satan in book V of *Paradise Lost* and compares it unfavourably to an inspissated quotation from Henry James's last, unfinished novel, *The Ivory Tower*. James, Eliot maintains, is complicated because he is reluctant 'to lose any of the real intricacies and by-paths of mental movement'. This is generally true of James, whose records of his characters' mental arithmetic are miracles of conscientiousness. It is not, however, true of the passage quoted. Which cannot be parsed. It isn't intricate. It is a solid dredlock of thought.[1] Nor is Eliot right to stigmatise the speech of Satan as someone 'making a speech carefully prepared for him', since this suggests inflexibility and contrivance. In fact, Satan's speech is without artifice. It is a rodeo of affront and anger. Sense clings on for dear life from the first moment—the list of titles that ignites a breathless aria of offended precedence, as if Jane Austen's Sir Walter Elliot, poring over the Baronetage, had found his name omitted. The argumentative direction is constantly skewed by digressive elaboration. I have cordoned off with square brackets every spasm of painful expatiation. It is a speech that can barely keep up with its own interruptions:

> Thrones, Dominations, Princedoms, Virtues, Powers,
> [If these magnific Titles yet remain
> Not merely titular, since by Decree]
> Another now hath to himself engross't
> All Power, [and us eclipst under the name
> Of King anointed,] for whom all this [haste
> Of midnight march, and hurried] meeting here,
> [This only] to consult how we may best
> [With what may be devis'd of honours new]
> Receive him coming to receive from us
> [Knee-tribute yet unpaid,] prostration vile,
> [Too much to one, but double how endur'd,
> To one and to his image now proclaimed?']

This isn't measured complication and the considered exposition of a press release.[2] It is indignation speaking as unruly thoughts occur to it and demand their say. It is great dramatic poetry.

In 'The Music of Poetry' (1942), Eliot says 'I may often repeat what I have said before, and I may often contradict myself'. This is true. In 'The Social Function of Poetry' (1943), Eliot argues that 'real poetry survives not only a change of popular opinion but the complete extinction of interest in the issues with which the poet was passionately concerned'. In 'Charles Whibley' (1931), he argued, more plausibly, the opposite: 'Literary style is sometimes assigned almost magical properties, or is credited with being a mysterious preservative for subject-matter which no longer interests. This is far from being absolutely true. Style alone cannot preserve; only good style in conjunction with permanently interesting content can preserve.'

As for repetition, this is Eliot in 'Hamlet' expounding the idea of the 'objective correlative': 'a set of objects, a situation, a chain of events which shall be the formula of that *particular* emotion.' The objective correlative is one of those 'coinages' that Eliot, in 'Milton II', says 'have had a success in the world astonishing to their author'. But it is easy to see why this particular coinage is successful. Its scientism—with its misleading scientific connotation of 'formula'—is a rebuke to belle-lettrism. Yet, the idea is obvious. What Eliot means is that the emotion of a character should be bodied forth in the action—as we can see from his example of a successful objective correlative, namely the somnambulism of Lady Macbeth. Soliloquy won't do. *Hamlet* is full of soliloquy. The difficulty for *Hamlet* and Hamlet both is that the inner state itself is opaque, however much Hamlet expatiates—whereas, Lady Macbeth's guilt about Duncan's death is lucid. Eliot wants something that will show, rather than tell—Lady Macbeth washing her hands—especially when the telling in *Hamlet* is so occluded and his emotion so powerful, *unparticular,* and unfocused.[3]

If Eliot's objective correlative is restricted to drama, it becomes the playwright's alternative to the soliloquy as a method of staging, of bodying forth, psychology. But, even in his *Hamlet* essay, Eliot addresses the larger problem of writing emotion. And not just simple emotion like Lady Macbeth's guilty conscience. How, he asks, do you write about 'the intense feeling, ecstatic or terrible, without an object or exceeding its object, [that] is something which every person of sensibility has known'? We need to be very clear about why Eliot thinks *this* is related to the staging of other, simpler emotions. Why is he conflating the two kinds of emotion? The key phrase is 'without an object or exceeding its object'—which makes it *sound* as if it lacks an objective correlative. But the problem here is not an artistic one at all. It is the problem of feeling an emotion you do not understand because it is without an adequate cause. This is a very special case indeed (even though Eliot attributes it to 'every person of sensibility'). Eliot argues that the artist uses 'his ability to intensify the world to his emotions'. He creates a set of events, a situation, that will correspond to this extraordinary emotion—be its objective correlative. Whereas before the objective correlative staged an emotion, made it manifest, so the audience could read it, in this special case the events of the play are almost a form of therapy, a reading, an interpretation, of the original inexplicable emotion. In the first case, the audience is to be shown something. In the second case, it is the artist who learns something about himself. As a theory, the second half is conceived by the bold, exploratory conceptualist—by Eliot the astronaut.

In 'The Social Function of Poetry' (1945), without naming it, Eliot revisits the site of this second 'psychological' objective correlative. Listing various functions of poetry, Eliot mentions 'the expression of something we have experienced but have no words for, which enlarges our consciousness or refines our sensibility'. This is the core of his argument in this essay—that, without expression, our emotions will atrophy. The poet's role is to find objective expression for the purely subjective. The poet articulates the inexpressible—and makes the culture more articulate and, therefore, more sensible to subtle feeling. This is quite different from the idea of the objective correlative as restricted to drama.

Put like this, the objective correlative looks more intelligible—a refinement of the idea of impersonality[4] in art. Every artist starts with his emotions and his autobiography—and addresses the task of transcending mere subjectivity. Self-expression isn't the sole aim. The aim is to create an intelligible work of art. The two functions of the objective correlative—to make emotion manifest for a theatre audience; to articulate one's inexplicable feelings—are conjoined a little uncomfortably, like unidentical Siamese twins.

Eliot's coat-trailing verdict on *Hamlet*—'the play is most certainly an artistic failure'—is fatally circular in its argument. The circularity, though, is disguised by his 'exposition' of the suggestive neologism, 'objective correlative'. When a play succeeds, it is because the dramatist's emotional raw materials are externalised successfully. Lady Macbeth's guilt is manifest in her sleepwalking. Inner emotional states—Antony's infatuation with Cleopatra, Coriolanus's pride—are borne out by the stage events. When a play fails, this doesn't happen: 'the artistic "inevitability" lies in this complete adequacy of the external to the emotion; and this is precisely what is deficient in *Hamlet*.' Coldly summarised, Eliot's argument is that *Hamlet* is a failure because it does not succeed.

In his 1944 lecture on Johnson, Eliot is clear about the relationship between a poet's criticism and his poetry: 'we can only understand a poet's criticism of poetry in relation to the poetry which he writes.' The essay on *Hamlet* is iconoclastic and incoherent in equal measure—consistently, unhelpfully, Eliot conflates the play with its protagonist. But it dramatically illuminates Eliot's poetic preoccupations with the nature of 'difficult' emotion. As a classicist, he is interested in fugitive and unusual emotions because they are so different from the standard powerful emotions of romantic literature. The last two pages of his *Hamlet* essay expound, not Shakespeare's play, but Eliot's own poetic agenda.

Eliot is interested in the emotion that is 'inexpressible'—not just here, but everywhere. In his lecture on Johnson, he identifies Johnson's prejudice in favour of 'sense' and meaning, and addresses its opposite, the idea of rhapsody, 'melodious raving', the 'permanent appetite of humanity for an occasional feast of drums and cymbals'. And in parenthesis, Eliot touches on his own central idea: 'there is poetry which represents an attempt to extend the confines of the human consciousness and to report of things unknown, to express the inexpressible.' In 'The Music of Poetry' (1942), he writes: 'the poet is occupied with frontiers of consciousness beyond which words fail, though meanings still exist.' If we ask where this central idea comes from, the answer is that it comes from Matthew Arnold's 'The Buried Life'. The objective correlative, in the nondramatic sense, is an account of the artist straining to objectify and embody his subjective inner murk—his buried life.

In ' "Rhetoric" and Poetic Drama', with his characteristic analytic rigour and comprehensive citation of instances, Eliot tries to define 'rhetoric' as more than merely bad writing. He finally settles for a 'rhetoric of substance'—by which he means the overblown *as an aspect of characterisation*. This is the kind of subtle emotion that interests the young Eliot—Shakespeare staging a character's sense of his own dramatic possibilities.[5] In Shakespeare, Eliot argues, there is great rhetoric—when Shakespeare makes his characters *indulge* in rhetoric. Richard II is the obvious example of the self-dramatising character, though Eliot doesn't invoke him. He prefers the idea of Othello, at once tragic and tinged with self-pity, in his final oratorical speech. Eliot's point is that rhetoric, oratory, can sometimes be realistic. In real life we act, we see ourselves dramatically. This is shrewd, subtle, observant, and true. Think of Prufrock's thespian modesty—his refusal of the main role, 'not Prince Hamlet', but 'an attendant lord'.

In ' "Rhetoric" and Poetic Drama', Eliot says of poetic drama: 'it must take genuine and substantial human emotions, such emotions as observation can confirm, typical emotions, and give them artistic form.' In 1919, then, Eliot appears to be leery of obscure emotion. In particular, he mistrusts Maeterlinck, whose emotions are inarticulate because they are insubstantial, 'not significant enough to endure full daylight'. Which is what he partially says, in the same year, in the *Hamlet* essay—that Shakespeare fails because the emotion he is attempting to articulate is recherché. Yet, as I have already said, recherché emotions, the inexpressible emotions, are what draw him as a writer. In other words, he is effectively contradicting himself.

The choice is between the comprehensible approach to emotions and the comprehensive approach to emotions. Eliot's contradiction, his conflict, is apparent in the closing remarks of his *Hamlet* essay, when he evokes Jules Laforgue: 'the Hamlet of Laforgue is an adolescent; the Hamlet of Shakespeare is not.' In other words, we *understand* Laforgue because we understand adolescence, but Eliot is interested in more than the exaggerated, easily ironised emotions of adolescence. He is leaving Laforgue, his earliest influence, behind. With Laforgue, we know where we are, whereas 'Shakespeare attempted to express the inexpressibly horrible'—'which proved too much for him.' Though presented as a counsel of despair, Eliot's ambition declares itself in his final sentence: 'we should have to understand things which Shakespeare did not understand himself.'

The objective correlative, the dissociation of sensibility, the auditory imagination, the frontiers of consciousness, the idea that great poets steal, or that great poetry can communicate before it is understood, or that the meaning of a poem is 'somewhere between the writer and the reader'. These are radical hypotheses and formulations that Eliot stigmatised, in 'The Frontiers of Criticism' (1956), as 'a few notorious phrases which have had a truly embarrassing success in the world'. This is too modest, though it is true that sometimes Eliot *refined* his more radical, more vulnerable formulations. And it is also true that some shouldn't be taken at face value.

I take my lead from Eliot who was himself a prompt deflationist. Think of his drily comic incredulity as he lets the air out of I. A. Richards's 'Spiritual Exercises': 'I cannot see why the facts of birth and of death should appear odd in themselves, unless we have a conception of some other way of coming into the world and of leaving it, which strikes us as more natural.' And I love his flat, Johnsonian rejection, also in *The Use of Poetry*, of Coleridge's famous distinction between fancy and imagination. 'If, as I have already suggested, the difference between imagination and fancy amounts in practice to no more than the difference between good and bad poetry, have we done more than take a turn round Robin Hood's barn?' (The same objection could be levelled at Hopkins's undergraduate formulation of 'Parnassian'.)

To turn to Eliot's suspect formulations, in his essay on the Elizabethan dramatist Philip Massinger, he famously asserts that 'immature poets imitate; mature poets steal; bad poets deface what they take, and good poets make it into something better, or at least something different'. This is lifted, wittily, from George Saintsbury's essay on Laurence Sterne's *Tristram Shandy*: 'the charge of plagiarism is usually an excessively idle one; for when a man of genius steals, he always makes the thefts his own; and when a man steals without genius, the thefts are mere fairy gold which turns to leaves and pebbles under his hand.' A *jeu*, then, which has been elected into the academy.

Equally over-prized is Eliot's much-cited contention, in his essay on Dante, that 'genuine poetry can communicate before it is understood'. You can see why this might be useful if you are a modernist whose meaning isn't as quickly available as, say, A. E. Housman's. Yet in its entirety, Eliot's hypothesis contains a fatal reservation (in parenthesis) that renders it nugatory. 'It is a test (a positive test, I do not assert that it is always valid negatively), that genuine poetry can communicate before it is understood.' This means that genuine poetry *sometimes* communicates before it is understood—and sometimes not. If it doesn't 'communicate' before it is understood, it may still be genuine poetry. As a 'test', its usefulness is dramatically limited. Just suppose for a second that it was a pregnancy test. And what does Eliot mean by 'communicate'? Is communication possible without understanding? If you do not speak a language, you may communicate by bodily gesture—smiling or tearing your hair—because these gestures are understood. But without *any* understanding, no communication is possible. You are in Tbilisi airport. You don't speak Georgian. An announcement in Georgian on the (expressionless, unsmiling) public address system tells you that your luggage has gone to Riga rather than Heathrow. At that moment, you won't get the joke. You won't see the funny side until much later.

Since the Romantics, the idea of a split between thought and feeling has been a commonplace—'wise passiveness' and the elevation of the heart over the brain's mere reasoning. For our purposes, Wordsworth's 'The Tables Turned' can provide an epitome: 'One impulse from a vernal wood / May teach you more of man, / Of moral evil and of good / Than all the sages can.' As an anti-Romantic, Eliot deplored this fissure between thought and feeling. The classicist regretted the rejection of intellect—and sought to account for it. Hence the coinage, in 'The Metaphysical Poets' (1921), of 'dissociation of sensibility'—which is a new name to designate (and deplore) the inception of an old set of circumstances. Eliot was brilliant at giving a dogma a good name. The theory proposes—not the preference you might expect—but a time when thought and feeling were unified. The division between intellect and sensibility, the 'dissociation', took place some time between (roughly) 1635 and 1832—between 'the time of Donne or Lord Herbert of Cherbury and the time of Tennyson and Browning'.

Over a period of two hundred years, then, 'something' 'happened to the mind of England'. The mind of England changed its mind, its way of thinking. Very gradually. The slowness is comforting. Anything speedier might seem implausible, since 'the mind of England' must be made up of all the individual minds in England. For those minds to renounce one way of thinking (so emphatically, so unanimously) for another way of thinking would have to be a very gradual process. Historically, unanimity isn't something one expects of the mind of England—not when you think of the Civil War, the Whigs as the party of the Protestant succession, Catholics suffering their civil disabilities, and the rise of the aptly named Dissenters. Epistemology, though, is more malleable than history. Hence the pinpoint accuracy of Eliot's two-hundred-year chronology. In 'Thoughts after Lambeth' (1931), Eliot is rightly scornful of the Lambeth Conference, let alone 'the mind of England', and the idea of 'three hundred bishops' pooling their views:

'Let us imagine (if we can imagine such persons agreeing to that extent) the fatuity of an encyclical letter produced by the joint efforts of Mr. H. G. Wells, Mr. Bernard Shaw and Mr. Russell; or Professors Whitehead, Eddington and Jeans; or Dr. Freud, Dr. Jung and Dr. Adler; or Mr. Murry, Mr. Fausset, the Huxley Brothers and the Reverend Dr. Potter of America.' The otiose capitalisation of 'Brothers' is clearly designed to summon up the Marx Brothers—and is an index of Eliot's contempt for the fatuity of consensus.

Eliot's theory is surely a myth—as exciting as it is unprovable, almost Wildean in its sacrifice of rigour to éclat. And isn't the Fall subconsciously feeding this myth of knowledge? There, only two creatures have to fall and everyone suffers the consequences. The 'mind of England' is a high-sounding but bogus entity, argumentatively endangered as soon as you consider the chasm between, say, the reader of the *Sun* and the Warton Professor of English at the University of Oxford. The gap may not be as large as you think, but it is sufficient to make us doubt the idea of *the* mind of England.

Unsurprisingly, when Eliot revisits his theory in 'Milton II' (1947), we witness, in Martin Amis's memorable phrase, a Tour de France of backpedalling. The phrase 'retains some validity', we learn—a validity that is strictly hypothetical: '*If* such a dissociation did take place . . . ' [my italics]. The visionary astronaut has given way to the harassed accountant evasively defending an obvious case of tax evasion: 'All we can say is, that something like this did happen; that it had something to do with the Civil War; that it would even be unwise to say it was caused by the Civil War, but that it is a consequence of the same causes which brought about the Civil War; that we must seek the causes in Europe, not in England alone; and for what these causes were, we may dig and dig until we get to a depth at which words and concepts fail us.' If you took this fraudulent flannel of Eliot's and translated it into body language, you'd see Mr. Merdle, Dickens's dubious financier, taking his own wrists into custody.

The 'auditory imagination' is another improbable theoretic construct—an intellectual improvisation designed to patronise Matthew Arnold's ear. Arnold was an irksome intellectual mentor, to whom Eliot owed his ironic manner, his lofty amused judiciousness, an 'Indian detachment', and a disposition to classicist precepts. At the end of his essay on Arnold in *The Use of Poetry*, Eliot defines the auditory imagination as follows:

> what I call the 'auditory imagination' is the feeling for syllable and rhythm, penetrating far below the conscious levels of thought and feeling, invigorating every word; sinking to the most primitive and forgotten, returning to the origin and bringing something back, seeking the beginning and the end. It works through meanings, certainly, or not without meanings in the ordinary sense, and fuses the old and obliterated and the trite, the current, and the new and surprising, the most ancient and the most civilised mentality.

This auditory imagination has been with us so long—since 1933—that we feel assured of its existence and shocked to think it might only have the status of a discarded concept like the fancy. Eliot had a wonderful ear, but this auditory imagination is really an aural Swiss army knife invented, conjured up, to patronise the obvious music of Arnold's poetry. In 'Sohrab and Rustum' and in 'Dover Beach' there are very fine, lucid sound effects—Arnold's description of the 'shorn and parcelled Oxus' as 'a foiled circuitous wanderer', or the sea and 'its melancholy, long, withdrawing roar' with the drag of the shingle passed from 'draw' to 'roar'. However, Eliot isn't interested in being fair to Arnold. He owes him too much. Therefore, he invents a faculty that penetrates 'far below the conscious levels of thought and feeling', then implies that he, Eliot, possesses this gift, while Arnold does not. We should hang on to our common sense. If the auditory imagination operates 'far below the conscious levels of thought and feeling', it is, of course, irrefutable. Yet if it is 'far below the conscious levels of thought and feeling'—yet another buried life— how is it that Eliot can provide us with such a detailed account of its mystical operations?

The answer is probably the work of F. Max Müller. Eliot has assimilated the poet to the philologist. It is as if Max Müller's scholarship had eloped with Coleridge's secondary imagination as defined in *Biographia Literaria*. Eliot's auditory imagination is a romantic union, a fantastic pairing, a chimera, a hybrid. Like Coleridge's secondary imagination, it 'dissolves, diffuses, dissipates, in order to recreate' and at the same time romantically declares (in Max Müller's formulation) that: 'every word, as soon as we hear it, carries us off to near and distant memories. They float about us like thin gossamer filaments in autumn.' When Müller gives an example, though, it serves only to show how comparatively impoverished, how amateurish, how unscholarly Eliot's auditory imagination must be without specialist knowledge spanning several languages:

> in Sanskrit this root helps us to express cattle, pa*s*u, which is the Latin *pecus*, Gothic *faihu*, German *vieh*, cattle; also *pecunia* and *pecus*, our lawyer's *fee*. It supplies, besides, pa*s*a, fetter, and similar words. Now, when we have a word for animal, such as *pecus*,

we have also the material for expressing such concepts as *peculiar*, the transition of meaning being clear enough from *peculium*, one's private property, to *peculiaris*, anything that is one's own—anything that is proper, singular, individual, and, it may be, odd. It is difficult to resist the siren songs of language, and not to follow her into all her flights of imagination.

That last breathless declaration may be the germ of Eliot's newfound mental faculty.

Strangely enough, in 'Milton I', only a couple of years later, Eliot again mentions the auditory imagination. Now, though, it isn't an essential component of the poet's art—sadly lost to Matthew Arnold—so much as a disability—an affliction suffered by the blind Milton and the visually impaired Joyce. Its symptoms are thinness of visual imagery and a depletion of meaning: 'the hypertrophy of the auditory imagination at the expense of the visual and tactile, so that inner meaning is separated from the surface, and tends to become something occult'. In two years, this formerly prized poetic asset has become a liability—as it is once more pressed contradictorily into service against another poet whose work Eliot dislikes.

Throughout this study, I have argued for Arnold as Eliot's powerful, repressed father figure. In his essay on Pascal, Eliot notes that Montaigne was a writer repugnant to Pascal, a writer Pascal set out to demolish—and a writer whose influence is omnipresent. 'Yet, in the *Pensées*, at the very end of [Pascal's] life, we find passage after passage, and the slighter they are the more significant, almost "lifted" out of Montaigne, down to a figure of speech or a word.' In the same way, when Eliot decides that Whitman is a great *prose* writer, we recall Arnold on Dryden and Pope as 'classics of our prose'. Examples could be easily multiplied. In *Cul-*

ture and Anarchy, Arnold's version of the rioter—hooting as he likes, threatening as he likes, smashing where he likes—provides Eliot with his analogue for the Inner Voice in 'The Function of Criticism', as he acknowledges: 'The inner voice, in fact, sounds remarkably like an old principle which has been formulated by an elder critic in the now familiar phrase of "doing as one likes".' When Eliot coins the neologism 'polyphiloprogenitive' in 'Mr Eliot's Sunday Morning Service', we recall Arnold's 'philoprogenitiveness' in 'Our Liberal Practitioners'. Would Eliot have written *Notes towards the Definition of Culture* without the prior example of *Culture and Anarchy*? Or 'The Function of Criticism' without Arnold's 'The Function of Criticism'? Their relationship is situated uncomfortably between conversation and argument. It is fundamentally oppositional. And it is also, on Eliot's side, indebted. One central argument of *After Strange Gods* is the frailty of the individual opinion as against some seat of external authority. Clearly, this disposition in favour of authority derives from Arnold's preference for a literary academy and his adjudication between dissenters and the established church.

If they share so much, why then this standoff? The religious Eliot dislikes Arnold because he thinks Arnold is a humanist, who believes that religion is a body of moral doctrine—rather than an encounter with God. As for humanists, Eliot is prepared to accept T. E. Hulme's summary: 'the refusal to believe any longer in the radical imperfection of either Man or Nature.' To the humanist, man is not fallen; he merely needs counselling.

Eliot's criticism provides us with yet another connection. In 'Milton II', Eliot remarks wryly that 'one or two phrases of my coinage . . . have had a success in the world astonishing to their author'. We have listed them and discussed them. The objective correlative, dissociation of sensibility, the auditory imagination. One could do the same for Arnold, who is Eliot's exemplar in this, as in many other things. Naturalistic interpretation, moral interpretation, the application of noble ideas to life, sweetness and light, machinery, Barbarians, Hellenism, Hebraism, the grand style. Eliot may claim, in his essay on F. H. Bradley, that Arnold's 'best phrases remain forever gibing and scolding in our memory', but those best phrases 'gibe' and 'scold' rather than fascinate and achieve indispensability. Arnold was less lucky than Eliot in his reception. His intellectual shorthand irritated his audience.

> Nothing has raised more questioning among my critics than these words, *noble, the grand style.* People complain I do not define these words sufficiently, that I do not tell enough about them. 'The grand style, but what *is* the grand style?' they cry; some with an inclination to believe in it, but puzzled; others mockingly and with incredulity. Alas! The grand style is the last matter in the world for verbal definition to deal with adequately.

Actually, Arnold defines and amplifies, defines and amplifies— but his catchphrases were catchphrases that irritated more than they caught on. Partly because he *could* define them. Eliot was cannier—as he records in his Dante essay: 'I wish to make clear that my own opinions are opinions founded only upon reading the text. I do not think they are such as can either be verified or refuted by scholars; I mean to restrict my comments to the unprovable and the irrefutable.'

His great critical genius, I believe, is not in the area of the unprovable, but in his criticism of individual authors and the occasional flash of helpless, counterintuitive, fearless brilliance: in 'Wilkie Collins and Dickens': 'But the frontier of drama and melodrama is vague; the difference is largely a matter of emphasis; perhaps no drama has ever been greatly and permanently successful without a large melodramatic element.' Breathtaking. Discuss.

Appendix 1

ELIOT AND
ANTI-SEMITISM

'I AM NOT AN ANTI-SEMITE AND NEVER HAVE BEEN', Eliot insisted. 'It is a terrible slander on a man.'[1] Eliot himself, then, knew precisely what was at stake. Anti-Semitism is a charge of the utmost gravity. And it was levelled at Eliot periodically throughout his career— and has been after his death.

In 1958, an anonymous reviewer in the *Times Literary Supplement* accused Eliot of sympathies with fascism and anti-Semitism. Eliot convincingly disposed of the charge of fascist sympathies and asked for evidence of his anti-Semitism. The reviewer (Burns Singer) was silent. On 6 September 1958, Christopher Logue simply listed what he (and many others) have considered self-evident examples of anti-Semitism in Eliot's work. Eliot responded: 'Your correspondent Christopher Logue has supported the accusations of your reviewer with all but two of the pieces of "evidence" which those who share his frame of mind are wont to produce against me.' And Eliot does not deign to address them.

Some have thought that Eliot misused his accumulated authority and seniority against a relatively unknown young writer—by not answering the specific charges and instead dismissing them on the grounds that these were the 'usual' passages cited against him. But this cannot be the explanation of Eliot's refusal to answer, because their exchange was public. Had their exchange been in private, it might have been an explanation—Eliot the icon, as it were, simply turning on his heel, refusing to condescend to answer someone he regarded as a cultural inferior, a snob delivering a snub. As it was, however, to those for whom the 'evidence' of anti-Semitism was self-evident, Eliot appeared not authoritative, but evasive.

But perhaps Eliot merely meant that these examples were so flimsy in his view as not to require any answer. They were not evidence, but 'evidence'. Which is odd when, even to sympathetic critics, they seem at points to overlap with anti-Semitism. What is the explanation? To those already convinced of Eliot's anti-Semitism, the explanation is simple. Eliot was avoiding the issue.

This cannot be the case, however. Were Eliot bent on shielding his past, on avoiding the issue, why would he have *solicited* the list of charges in the first place? I think this is the behaviour of an innocent person. The innocent person knows proof cannot be found. I don't think it is possible to argue that Eliot was merely responding as any guilty person would—with the desperate cry of 'prove it'. The guilty person hopes proof will not be found. The analogy is false, a poor fit, because, as Eliot knew, the 'evidence' cited by Logue was in the public domain anyway. It was to be found in his published work.

I suggest the following alternative explanation for his refusal to answer the charges. He was genuinely convinced of his own innocence. For him, there was no case to answer.[2] Therefore the incriminating cluster of apparent instances of intolerance will not have felt so to Eliot. For him, these references are scattered across long periods of time—months, years—so their concentration will not have seemed a concentration to him. They will not have felt like a programme or the anti-Jewish agenda that Anthony Julius wishes to attribute to him. The grouping together and the adversarial interpretations must have seemed malicious.

A covert anti-Semite might disguise his views while promulgating them. An extreme anti-Semite would be unambiguous and full frontal. Once assume that inner certainty of innocence, and it isn't difficult to see why Eliot didn't see the 'obvious' anti-Semitic readings. Or take pains to eliminate them. If he felt utterly without prejudice, he wouldn't take care to be wary of anti-Semitic interpretation.

My grounds for seeing if Eliot can be defended—and I think he can be—are as follows. His reaction to Logue's list in the *Times Literary Supplement*—a list Eliot solicited himself—allows for the interpretation that he *felt* himself innocent, not merely that he declared himself innocent. In 1941, he spoke out against anti-Semitism in the *Christian Newsletter*.

Lastly, there is a central argumentative equivocation in Anthony Julius's account of Eliot's anti-Semitism. Julius argues that Eliot is an invigorator of anti-Semitic clichés—an argument that presumes Eliot was an open anti-Semite. Which he manifestly wasn't because Julius's book, *T. S. Eliot, Anti-Semitism, and Literary Form* (1996), *argues* for Eliot's anti-Semitism. Were Eliot openly anti-Semitic, such an argument would be unnecessary. Therefore, Eliot must be a covert anti-Semite. But if that is the case, how can he be an *invigorator* of anti-Semitic clichés? Julius might have been on surer ground had he argued for a third possibility—unconscious, visceral anti-Semitism in Eliot. There remains the possibility that Eliot was neither a covert, nor an overt anti-Semite, but a man very occasionally guilty of sporadic, unconsidered anti-Semitism, which he would strenuously deny if asked to consider his position. As he did.

My own position is reserved. We do not have all the evidence. There may be things in the correspondence. Eliot's sense of his own innocence may be vivid, but no one can remember his whole life.

Of course, it is simpler to convict Eliot of anti-Semitism—a verdict which appeals to our contemporary instinct for what Milan Kundera has eloquently called 'criminography', by which he means the desire to arraign artists on exclusively moral grounds, the desire to annihilate rather than administer complicated justice, the desire to consider only the faults and ignore the virtues and the achievements. Eliot knew all about what he called 'seductive simplicity'—'the direct and persuasive appeal to intellect and emotions' that is likely to be 'altogether more plausible than the truth'. My own instinct is for complication.

Nearly a decade earlier than Anthony Julius, Christopher Ricks also examined the charges of anti-Semitism laid against Eliot in his book *T. S. Eliot and Prejudice* (1988). Ricks found that there was some truth in the charges but entered a plea of mitigation because Eliot's poem *Little Gidding* expressed a general regret for 'things ill done and done to others' harm / Which once you took for exercise of virtue'—lines which Ricks took to be a reference to Eliot's anti-Semitism, obliquely expressed. Julius will have none of this. Throughout his book, he maintains a formal position that he admires Eliot's poetry, but his use of the evidence is candidly adversarial. His Eliot is not simply an anti-Semite but also a racist and a misogynist.

Here is my reading of the usual examples.

1. The *Yellow Spot* review

Anthony Julius, C. K. Stead, Christopher Ricks, Ronald Bush, Tom Paulin, James Fenton, and Louis Menand have all assumed that Eliot wrote the review of *The Yellow Spot* (1936, the first documentary account of mistreatment of German Jews) that appeared unsigned in *The Criterion*. For them, this was a crucial piece of evidence—though they had no way, apparently, of knowing if Eliot wrote it. This makes it inadmissible evidence.

In any case, the review is not anti-Semitic. It argues that the treatment of Jews is deplorable: 'certainly no English man or woman would wish to be a German Jew in Germany today.' But it questions the right of other nations to 'moral dictatorship'—and sees no practical course of action to 'alleviate the situation of those whose misfortunes it describes'. Moral condemnation is ineffectual. It notes, too, that the book is undecided between 'extermination' and 'persecution'. One can agree with Anthony Julius that it assuredly 'understates the seriousness of the book's subject matter, while overstating its defects', without accepting that it is anti-Semitic.

Nor was the review written by Eliot, despite the scholarly consensus. In due course, Valerie Eliot, the poet's widow, having examined the financial records of the magazine, identified the author of the contested review as Montgomery Belgion. Julius had written that, if he were wrong in attributing the authorship to Eliot, he would have done him an 'injustice'. His subsequent letter to the *Times Literary Supplement* conceded nothing in the way of apology, but instead complained that scholars were at the mercy of the poet's widow. Why, he wanted to know, hadn't this fact been disclosed before now? Alas for Julius, the very next day a letter was printed in the *London Review of Books* pointing out that Mrs Eliot's research was not strictly necessary, since book reviewers were identified in the index of *The Criterion*.

All the scholars had to do was consult the index.

None of them had done so.

Instead, they had used against Eliot an unsigned review for which there was no evidence of Eliot's authorship. The unwarranted prominence given to *The Yellow Spot* review demonstrates a determination to convict the poet of anti-Semitism, which itself verges on the prejudicial. Ironically, the 'anti-Semitic' author of *The Yellow Spot* review is the identical Montgomery Belgion who, in the last number of Eliot's *Criterion,* though an admirer of Charles Maurras in certain respects, singled out for specific criticism Maurras's Action Française as 'rabidly anti-Jewish'. There is comedy in the gaffe, of course, but it is profoundly disturbing that *so* many reputable critics should have admitted as evidence in the first place something so demonstrably flimsy.[3]

Nor is Eliot responsible for the piece because he was the editor. Ask any literary editor how responsible they are for the content of reviews commissioned. Julius's position—the only one now possible for him—is that 'Eliot's willingness to publish this ugly review suggests that he was blind to the martyrdom of German Jewry'.

2. The footnote in *Notes towards the Definition of Culture*

Since Eliot's death, George Steiner has been a persistent critic of Eliot's anti-Semitism. In particular, Steiner's disquiet has focused on a footnote in *Notes towards the Definition of Culture*. In 1948, Eliot wrote the footnote in *Notes towards* which (according to Steiner) implies that the Jews were somehow responsible for their fate: 'Nothing in Pound's black silliness equals the footnote in the *Notes Towards a [sic] Definition of Culture* in which Eliot, after Auschwitz, suggests, with feline caution, that the Jews did have some historical responsibility for the fate just visited upon them.'[4] In fact, there are *two* footnotes—the original footnote and the same footnote openly re-written by Eliot in 1962 to clarify his meaning.

On the first version of the footnote it is not difficult to project the ghost of Steiner's accusation. Not difficult to project the *ghost* of Steiner's accusation, but harder to inject any substance. Here is the original footnote:

> Since the diaspora, and the scattering of Jews amongst peoples holding the Christian Faith, it may have been unfortunate both for these peoples and for the Jews themselves, that the culture-contact between them has had to be within the neutral zones of culture in which religion could be ignored: and the effect may have been to strengthen the illusion that there can be culture without religion.

Steiner's interpretation of the original, unrevised footnote is stupid, in any case. Only someone *begging* for trouble would, in 1948, imply the Holocaust was the fault of the Jews. You would have not only to be malignant, but also a complete fool. Steiner imputes to Eliot 'feline caution'. No one would say such a thing in 1948, even with 'feline caution'.

By rewriting it, though, Eliot eliminates Steiner's interpretation. It becomes untenable:

> It seems to me highly desirable that there should be close cul-
> ture-contact between devout and practising Christians and de-
> vout and practising Jews. Much culture-contact in the past has been
> within those neutral zones of culture in which religion can be ig-
> nored, and between Jews and Gentiles both more or less emanci-
> pated from their religious traditions. The effect may have been to
> strengthen the illusion that there can be culture without religion.
> In this context I recommend to my readers two books by Profes-
> sor Will Herberg published in New York: *Judaism and Modern
> Man* (Farrar, Straus and Cudahy) and *Protestant-Catholic-Jew*
> (Doubleday).

No one can say of this that Eliot is suggesting the Jews were his-
torically responsible for their own fate.

If Eliot could recast this passage for clarity, why didn't he re-
write the offending poems and the passage from *After Strange Gods*
listed by Christopher Logue in the *Times Literary Supplement*?
Because rewriting wouldn't look like clarification. It would look
like an admission of guilt. Which Eliot—on the evidence of his
reaction to Logue's list—did not feel. He felt rather that he had
been misread. Or just *not* read. Inadequate or adversarial readers
are not a reason to rewrite one's works.

This is James Wood in *The Broken Estate* on Eliot's capital-
isation of the lowercase 'jew' in 'Gerontion' in 1963: 'This emen-
dation is an admission of guilt. It was not Gerontion who changed
the typeface, but Eliot.' In *The Dry Salvages*, we encounter 'dead
negroes', though nowadays the convention is the capitalised 'Ne-
groes'. My word processor's spell-check underlines 'jew' and
'negro' as errors. Conventions change. My 1943 Everyman edi-
tion of *Huckleberry Finn* uses 'negro' in the 'Explanatory': 'the

Missouri negro dialect'. Other examples in Twain are hard to find since Huck habitually uses 'nigger'—a usage, then conventional in the South, that has caused a few self-righteous cretins to convict Twain of racism. The OED gives examples of 'Jew' in uppercase and lowercase. Shakespeare's First Folio has the uppercase 'Iew', but capitalisation in Elizabethan times is a lottery. In the Quarto, 'Iew' is also uppercase. In pro-Semitic *Ulysses* (*Trieste-Zürich-Paris*, 1914–1921), 'jew' is lowercase in Stephen's dialogue ('Lopez, his jew's heart') and Eglinton's dialogue ('Prove that he was a jew'). Though Stephen in 'Nestor' dissents from Deasy's anti-Semitism, Stephen and Eglinton could, of course, both be anti-Semites. Bloom, however, cannot and yet he says: 'Christ was a jew like me.'

3. Free-thinking Jews and *After Strange Gods*

Anthony Julius opens his prosecution case by citing a famous instance of presumed anti-Semitism in Eliot's work, from *After Strange Gods*, the 1933 Page-Barbour lectures given by Eliot at the University of Virginia. The crucial passage is this:

> the population should be homogeneous; where two or more cultures exist in the same place they are likely either to be fiercely self-conscious or both to become adulterate. What is still more important is unity of religious background; and reasons of race and religion combine to make any large number of free-thinking Jews undesirable. There must be a proper balance between urban and rural, industrial and agricultural development. And a spirit of excessive tolerance is to be deprecated.

Though these four sentences are in their entirety an unfortunate collocation, for which Eliot has been properly harried over the years, it is that last sentence which particularly sticks in the craw of Christopher Ricks in *T. S. Eliot and Prejudice* (1988). 'Excessive tolerance' is a subheading in chapter 2, 'Anti-Semitism'. Ricks interprets this to mean Eliot is advocating intolerance: 'for this allows him to promise a dishonourable pardon to those who act out their intolerance, while not himself being openly inflammatory since his way of putting it maintains nothing.' A covert encouragement to intolerance, therefore, masked by the word 'excessive', which Professor Ricks finds circular or vacant.

But suppose for a charitable moment that Eliot meant exactly what he said. Suppose that the word 'excessive' was neither circular nor vacant, but carried the meaning it normally does. Consider this sentence: 'Excessive consumption of alcohol is to be deprecated.' Does this imply a need for total prohibition? No. It implies that alcohol should be consumed in moderation. 'And a spirit of excessive tolerance is to be deprecated.' Professor Ricks sees this as a covert incitement to intolerance. He is wrong. It is rather a passage that allows for limited numbers of free-thinking Jews—not 'large number[s]'. The wording is unfortunate, but the intention behind it is not inflammatory. It is moderate. If we read this sentence literally, without prejudice, as advocating tolerance on a limited front, it clearly affects the way in which we read the previous troubling sentence—'reasons of race and religion combine to make any large number of free-thinking Jews undesirable'. What we readers would be left with then, is this—a sentence which advocates a *degree* of tolerance. Much as, say, both the main parties in the United Kingdom restrict immigration, while admitting a proportion of cases.[5]

As it happens, there is another piece of evidence in Eliot's defence that supports my reading of those problematic sentences. It has always been there in the text of *After Strange Gods*, but you would not see it if you were expecting to convict Eliot of anti-Semitism. And it is crucial and decisive, in this instance. The Page-Barbour lectures address the need (as Eliot sees it) to establish or revive 'a tradition and a way of life'. He defines tradition thus: 'all those habitual actions, habits and customs, from the most significant religious rite to our conventional way of greeting a stranger.' These things, Eliot maintains, 'represent the blood kinship of "the same people living in the same place".' Nowadays of course, even the mention of 'blood kinship' makes us understandably nervous. When James Fenton lectured, as Oxford Professor of Poetry in 1996, on Eliot's anti-Semitism[6], he drew attention to the quotation marks around the phrase '"the same people living in the same place"'. But he did not know where the quotation came from. He had not read Joyce's *Ulysses*. Or he had not read it recently enough. Nor had Tom Paulin, Professor Ricks, or Anthony Julius.

Eliot's definition of a nation comes from the 'Cyclops' episode of Joyce's great and famously tolerant novel. It is Leopold Bloom's definition of a nation, offered to the bigoted Citizen whose rampant anti-Semitism wishes to expel the Semite interloper from the Irish nation. Leopold Bloom is a free-thinking Jew. And his definition, which is also his defence of his right to live in Ireland, is a definition that the allegedly anti-Semitic Eliot is happy to share. This insight should give us pause, both specifically and generally. By consciously alluding to Leopold Bloom, and marking the allusion with inverted commas, Eliot effectively includes free-thinking Jews in his recipe for a unified culture.[7] Perhaps, after all, reluctantly, we can agree that Eliot's use of the word 'excessive' was neither vacuous, nor circular, but strictly accurate. So that this famous *locus* of Eliot's anti-Semitism in *After Strange Gods* can be seen as nothing of the kind—but rather a recipe for a society in which the existing culture would not be adulterated, nor subject to the secession of a substantial section.

If we accept this, I think we should be more inclined to accept also that Eliot meant what he said, when, in correspondence with J. V. Healy, he maintained that he was arguing the undesirability of 'free-thinkers of any race' in large numbers—and that free-thinking Jews are 'only a special case'. By this, Eliot means that, given the Diaspora, free-thinking Jews are less likely than free-thinking Christians to retain the vestiges of their religion. This is surely uncontroversial even if arguable. Free-thinking Christians in Europe do live, or did live, in a basically Christian culture.

In Louis Menand's (6 June 1996) *New York Review of Books* essay-review of Anthony Julius, Eliot's qualification, '*free-thinking* Jews', went missing by the end of the piece. It became 'the direct reference to the undesirabilty of Jews'. No reference either to the qualification 'any large number'. Menand, better informed and more temperate than Julius, conceded that anti-Semitism was 'a relatively minor aspect' of Eliot's thought: 'part of the reason it was so half-baked even as anti-Semitism was that Eliot didn't give much attention to it, and in most of the poetry and almost all of the literary criticism it fades into insignificance.' Nevertheless, Menand's methodology proved to be remarkably like that of Julius—guilt by association.

4. Guilt by Association

Menand tells us that Julius is heavily dependent on Leon Poliakov's four-volume *History of Anti-Semitism*—a rabid context, which, on the face of it, looks a mite improbable for T. S. Eliot, O.M. and Nobel Prize winner. Menand's essay is devoted to showing us how

Eliot comes to be of this company and in what way. Where Julius cites verbal echoes with little evidential rigour, Menand cites the incriminating company Eliot kept: Pound, John Quinn, Charles Maurras, and Viscount Lymington (Gerald Wallop, later the Earl of Portsmouth). The evidence here is circumstantial in the main. And it carries conviction only in so far as you believe that friendship and/or association entails the friend in sharing the opinions of his close circle in their entirety.

When I tell you that I am a close friend of James Fenton and that we disagree about Eliot's anti-Semitism, you will know how risky I consider this method of argument to be. Let me start with Viscount Lymington's *Famine in England* (1938), a book that (Menand tells us) Eliot praised in *The Criterion* 'at some length, though in vague terms'. Menand quotes a Lymington passage denouncing immigrants and 'the foreign invasion of London' that goes on to invoke Arthur Lane's classically anti-Semitic book *The Alien Menace*.

There is no evidence that Eliot read *The Alien Menace* or that he approved of it. Certainly, Lymington was no social democrat, but Menand seriously misrepresents his book, its analysis, and its probable appeal to Eliot. Lymington argues for an agricultural revival, the stockpiling of a year's food, the abolition of death duties on land—anything, in fact, that will make England more self-sufficient and therefore avoid a famine in the war he regards (rightly) as imminent. *Famine in England* undoubtedly spoke to the agrarian sentimentalist in Eliot whom we see in *After Strange Gods* praising unified, rooted culture, settled on the land and opposed to deracinated cosmopolitanism. Eliot's 'Commentary' (October 1938) draws these conclusions from Lymington: 'What is fundamentally wrong is the *urbanization of mind* of which I have previously spoken . . . It is necessary that the greater part of the population, of all classes (so long as we have classes), should be settled in the country and dependent upon it.'

Lymington *can* sound like Rachel Carson as he deplores 'reckless use of sulphate of ammonia, nitro chalk, potash and other salts', which kills off the natural soil bacteria. He invokes dust bowls, deserts, and deforestation caused by mismanagement of the land—and you begin to see that, for Eliot, the waste land was not merely an emblem of spiritual aridity: 'The desert is squeezed in the tube-train next to you, / The desert is in the heart of your brother'.[8] It was also a literal fact to be feared. Lymington invokes 'the old fertility legends of Adonis and Tammuz' as versions of good agricultural practice—the cycle of life, decay, and renewal, of earthworms and bacteria creating healthy humus. Lymington, too, tries to show us fear in a handful of dust. We think of Eliot as the quintessential urban poet but he is also a poet who finds the City 'unreal'. Several times in *Inventions of the March Hare*, Eliot touches on our impoverished commerce with the natural world: 'We hibernate among the bricks / And live across the window panes.' This nostalgic disposition is Arnoldian and nineteenth century, and it allows us to see how attractive aspects of Lymington's programme might be to Eliot. Lymington actually uses the phrase 'merry England' as he invokes 'the unhurried cycle of the soil' far from 'the noise, restlessness and rootlessness of towns'. It is the antithesis of the rootless transients in *The Waste Land* who 'go south in winter', whose nationality is uncertain ('Bin gar keine Russin . . .').

Politically, Lymington is well to the right: he fears communists, mistrusts foreigners, disapproves of Italian and German dictatorships, and, while he approves of leadership, his assertion that 'blood and soil rule at last' isn't a declaration of solidarity with German fascism's 'Blut und Boden'. Though he had an audience with Hitler, his faith in English breeding stock and English soil is a landowner's patriotism. In any case, Eliot is not responsible for Viscount Lymington's political opinions on the evidence adduced by Menand.

It is interesting that anti-Semitic acquaintances can be used as evidence of a putative anti-Semitism, but that the reverse procedure is laughed out of court. Eliot had a high regard for Marianne Moore. In her memoir of *The Dial*, she mentions that some rejected authors 'were so incurious in their reading as to accuse us of anti-Semitism'. Surely Marianne Moore should count in Eliot's favour? She doesn't. 'Some of my best friends are Jewish' has long been good for an incredulous laugh. *Why*, when the contrary, 'Some of my best friends are anti-Semites', does carry weight?

One of these friends was Ezra Pound, to whom Eliot writes (31 October 1917): 'Burnham [Viscount Burnham] is a Jew merchant, named Lawson (sc. Levi-sohn?).' Louis Menand's essay in the *New York Review of Books* (6 June 1996) alludes to this and to a correspondence between Eliot and his patron John Quinn, which was anti-Semitic in places—though the worst offender is clearly Quinn. Menand doesn't quote the offending letter to Quinn (12 March 1923) but in paraphrase the offence is identical to the Pound letter. Eliot complains about his Jewish publisher Horace Liveright and asks Quinn if he can't find Eliot a decent Christian publisher. Without the text, we cannot judge Eliot's tone. The crux, though, seems to be his use of the adjective 'Jew' rather than the adjective 'Jewish'—'Jew merchant' and 'Jew publisher'. We certainly register a distinction now. Was the distinction so marked in 1917? In 1923? The OED has no examples of 'Jewish' as an adjective between 1874 and 1925: '3. *attrib.* And *Comb.* a. *attrib.* or as *adj.* That is a Jew, Jewish, as *Jew boy, butcher, girl, man, pedlar, physician, trooper* (such expressions now mainly in offensive use but not originally opprobious).' James Fenton also told me privately that Sir Isaiah Berlin had had a correspondence with Eliot about anti-Semitism. I should like to read it, as well as the Quinn correspondence. At the moment, we have not assembled all the evidence. Julius's book is at best premature.

5. 'Gerontion', 'Burbank with a Baedeker: Bleistein with a Cigar'

The general point that arises from the unforeseen intervention of the free-thinking Leopold Bloom is that, just as it is fatal to misunderstand the use of quotation marks in *After Strange Gods*, so, when it comes to a consideration of Eliot's poetry, it is dangerous to pronounce, as Anthony Julius often does, from a position of partial comprehension. These are very difficult poems. Yet Julius is prepared to preface hostile readings of Eliot's poems thus: 'While the poem cannot be reduced to a resolvable riddle, its hostility to Jews is instantly recognisable'; 'whatever its interpretative obscurities . . . ' In other words: 'I do not understand this poetry but I know for a certainty it is anti-Semitic.'

But Julius has a lawyer's way with evidence. He knows how to present a damaging case. For instance, his book is prefaced with an epigraph that tells us how Eliot was summarily turned out of a house in South Africa when his hostess, a Jew, read the anti-Semitic lines in 'Burbank with a Baedeker: Bleistein with a Cigar'. In his introductory salvo, Julius refers again to the anecdote and says that he hopes 'to keep faith' with it. In a footnote, however, he does no such thing. There, more than two hundred pages away, he tells us that the quotation is, in fact, 'at best, a melodramatic and telescoped version of the truth'. The truth, apparently, is to be found in correspondence located in the Sarah Gertrude Millin Collection at the William Cullen Library at the University of Witwatersrand. While Julius supplies all this information, he doesn't tell us what the truth is. Perhaps because he didn't know precisely. He thanks a Lavinia Braun for 'this information'. His reader is left with a discrepancy between the symbolic epigraph and the bathetic disclaimer in the endnotes.

Julius would like us to think him adversarial but fair. Actually, I think he is often unfair. For instance, he maintains that Eliot learned from French culture that 'a vigorous anti-Semitism' was 'compatible with cordial salon relations with Jews'. The relevant endnote refers us to Edouard Roditi, whose testimony is pro-Eliot: 'he even suggested publishing . . . one of my overtly Jewish poems . . . he expressed to me on several occasions after 1933 his horror of the anti-Semitic outrages in Nazi Germany.' This behaviour, I submit, manifestly exceeds Julius's lukewarm description of it in the main text as hypocritical cordiality.

Or take Eliot on Marx. Julius finds Eliot's evocation of Marx as a 'Jewish economist' an example of 'insulting' anti-Semitism: 'Describing Marx as a "Jewish economist", when he was less than a Jew and more than an economist, is insulting.' Marx was a Jew indifferent to Judaism, if not hostile. Eliot's offending sentence reads in full: 'I never expected that Hegel, having been inverted by a Jewish economist for his own purposes, should come back again into the favour.' The 'Jewish economist' *is* odd but it is odd for a reason which is not anti-Semitic. Eliot is relishing an irony. Julius should recognise this because, thirty pages earlier, he provides the necessary information for a proper appreciation of the irony. Hegel was a noted anti-Semite. For Hegel, 'Judaism is . . . the fulfillment of ugliness'.[9]

I must, reluctantly, leave consideration of details, the proper weighing of each iota of evidence, and come to my general objection to Julius's methodology. Which is guilt by association. His thesis is that Eliot placed his great gifts at the service of anti-Semitism—that he invigorates the stale clichés bandied about by rabid anti-Semites. Inevitably, this places Eliot in criminal, pathological company and assumes an equation between the articulate Eliot and the most cruel excesses of anti-Semitic discourse. I think this unlikely because I believe Eliot to have been proud of his intellectual independence. Remember, it was Eliot who admired Henry James for possessing 'a mind so fine that no idea could violate it'. There are three allegedly anti-Semitic lines in 'Gerontion':

> My house is a decayed house,
> And the Jew squats on the window-sill, the owner,
> Spawned in some estaminet of Antwerp,
> Blistered in Brussels, patched and peeled in London.

Julius prefaces this quotation prejudicially: 'the passage breathes hate, the sibilants hissing scorn.' We are then told that the speaker, Gerontion, *in these lines*, is 'spitting at the Jew in this opening stanza'. Untrue. But Julius arrives at this baseless reading by asserting that 'the word these other words intimate is "spit"'. And he cites Shakespeare's *Merchant*—Antonio's spitting and Shylock's bitter complaint about being spat on. I do not see why. The neutral verb 'squats' does not seem intrinsically anti-Semitic. For instance, Kipling's Kim habitually rests 'knees to chin': 'said Kim affably, squatting in the shade beside the lama'. Or Tekla in

Conrad's *Under Western Eyes:* 'she had squatted down to put it [a small bowl] on the floor for the benefit of a large cat.' This demonstrably harmless word provokes Julius to cite examples from anti-Semitic discourse in which Jews are forced to squat because they suffer from leprosy. Nor is Julius slow to emphasise the excremental connotations of 'squat'.

The verb 'spawned', while hardly flattering, hardly supports Julius's extrapolation that Gerontion's Jew 'emerges as if from the swamp'. 'Spawn' implies large numbers, indiscriminate fertility—and, therefore, poverty. I do not think the Jew who owns the '*decayed* house' and perches on its windowsill is the anti-Semitic cliché of the affluent Jewish magnate. 'Spawn' does not necessarily imply the idea of swamps. It can be the milt of fish—freshwater fish. Mushrooms have spawn. As a verb, it can be neutral, as it is in Erasmus's *On Folly* (translator, Kennett): 'The curiosity of the Greeks spawned so many subtleties.' Limiting 'spawn' to swamps permit Julius to cite, at length, disgusting examples of anti-Semitic discourse that stigmatise Jews as leeches, frogs, 'swamp-life'. But they are not examples from Eliot. Their connection with Eliot is nugatory.

'Blistered', 'patched' and 'peeled', in Julius's account, these adjectives refer to smallpox, lupus, trachoma, favus, eczema, and scurvy. Whereas Eliot is surely characterising the deracination of its owner—Antwerp, Brussels, London—and his poverty—born into a large family in Antwerp; a foot-sore, hand-sore manual labourer in Brussels; then someone in London, wearing repaired clothing, working outdoors, and therefore sunburnt.

Read Eliot's lines again. Here is the central weakness of Julius's thesis about Eliot as the gifted *invigorator* of anti-Semitic cliché. The lines of Eliot quoted are anodyne, torpid, compared to the anthology amassed by Julius from outside the poetry. And if Eliot is the invigorator, then what is his anti-Semitic status in Julius's eyes? As we saw, he can hardly be a covert anti-Semite. Yet he clearly isn't an open, rabid anti-Semite. Julius settles for a fudge: 'Eliot was *not* a typical anti-Semite . . . Eliot was rather, in some sense, an *extraordinary* anti-Semite.' I wonder what the sense of 'in some sense' might be.

In an early essay, 'The Function of Criticism', Eliot deplores the kind of interpretative criticism that 'is always producing parts of the body from its pockets, and fixing them in place'. This is Julius's method—one of wholesale importation. Moreover, with 'Gerontion', Julius is forced to deny that the poem is a dramatic monologue—which it manifestly is—so that he can attribute the three lines of alleged anti-Semitism to Eliot directly. Julius can be a very inaccurate reader.[10]

When Julius comes to the infamous 'Burbank with a Baedeker: Bleistein with a Cigar', he once more, understandably, editorialises Eliot's words. Again, he is anxious to rule out the possibility that the poem is a dramatic monologue, with a loophole therefore through which the anti-Semitic Eliot could escape. On the other hand, he cannot resist the introduction of theatre because it improves his argument against Eliot. 'One *imagines* a pose being struck'; 'one *imagines* the sentence lispingly spoken' [my italics]. I imagine nothing of the kind. This is a difficult poem to defend. I myself have always thought the crucial lines indicative of Eliot's anti-Semitism: 'The rats are underneath the piles. / The Jew is underneath the lot.' I have changed my mind.

> . . . On the Rialto once.
> The rats are underneath the piles.

The Jew is underneath the lot.
Money in furs. The boatman smiles . . .

There is anti-Semitism here. But it is not Eliot's. It is Burbank's. It
has to be. The two crucial, middle lines are framed, fatally for Julius's
argument, by two incomplete phrases, 'On the Rialto once' and
'Money in furs', whose truncation, were we to encounter it in *Ulysses*,
would instantly indicate interior monologue. They would indicate
interior monologue anywhere, as a matter of fact, except in Eliot
when one reads prejudicially. Basically Burbank's anti-Semitism is
a public posture produced by a private derangement—Bleistein's
titular cigar, not mentioned in the poem, tells us that he has suc-
ceeded sexually with Princess Volupine where Burbank has failed.
    There is, I know, a difficulty still awaiting attention in the poem.

A lustreless protrusive eye
Stares from the protozoic slime
At a perspective of Canaletto.
The smoky candle end of time

Declines.

Following on the stanza describing Bleistein as seen by
Burbank—'A saggy bending of the knees / And elbows, with the
palms turned out'—these lines naturally attach to him, in a way
that is morally unacceptable. Julius envisages Bleistein in an art
gallery, *failing* to appreciate Canaletto (my italics, Julius's assump-
tion). I wish to propose a different reading—a reading that takes
'the smoky candle end of time' declining as a helpful explanatory
gloss on the preceding lines with their *metaphorical* 'protrusive
eye'. We are being offered not a disgusting example of anti-
Semitism, but rather a description of a sunset—the pale evening

sun sinking into the Venice lagoon and shining on architectural vistas often painted by Canaletto. (For the same figurative topos, compare Byron's *Beppo* stanza XLIII, in which Byron praises Venice for its invariable sunshine. Here, a non-Venetian sunrise is compared to an eye: 'I also like to dine on becaficas, / To see the Sun set, sure he'll rise tomorrow, / Not through a misty morning twinkling weak as / A drunken man's dead eye in maudlin sorrow . . . ') In other words, 'Burbank with a Baedeker: Bleistein with a Cigar' is not an anti-Semitic poem, but a poem about anti-Semitism. This new interpretation will seem implausible for a time, in the way that radical re-readings do before they become accepted.

A word, too, about the end of the poem. What is the answer to Burbank's question about the winged lion of Venice, the city's symbol? 'Who clipped the lion's wings / And flea'd his rump and pared his claws? / Thought Burbank . . . ' As the conclusion to *this* poem, the question is rhetorical. The answer it requires is: the Jews. Remember, the word 'ghetto' was coined in Venice, whose Jews lived where there was once a foundry for casting cannon. Originally, 'getto' meant to 'cast'. The word's meaning widened semantically and shifted to cover the restricted area in any city where Jews live. Venice, then, had a pronounced Jewish presence—and, therefore, thinks Burbank, a Jewish problem. '*Thought Burbank* . . . [my italics]'. *This* thought at least is definitely Burbank's. And, I would argue, contributes to my idea that much of the poem is Burbank's interior monologue—and that *all* of it is focalised for Burbank.

6. 'Dirge'

Full fathom five your Bleistein lies
Under the flatfish and the squids.

Graves' Disease in a dead jew's eyes!
When the crabs have eat the lids.
Lower than the wharf rats dive
Though he suffer a sea-change
Still expensive rich and strange.

The other piece of evidence singled out by Julius is the taste-less and distasteful 'Dirge' from *The Waste Land* manuscript. It describes the disintegration of Bleistein's drowned body—death by water—and the way it is preyed on by aquatic life. It is the strongest piece of evidence that Eliot was anti-Semitic and it is difficult to defend. It was, of course, off the record. After the discovery of *The Waste Land* manuscript, it took its place on the record. As I said, no one can remember the whole of his life. I doubt if Eliot remembered 'Dirge'. His recall of *The Waste Land* manuscript was always vague.

'Dirge' was presumably intended as a companion piece to 'Death By Water', in which we see the drowned Phlebas having his bones picked 'in whispers' by the sea current. 'Dirge' is intended to illustrate Eliot's coda: '*Gentile or Jew* / O you who turn the wheel and look to windward, / Consider Phlebas, who was once handsome and tall as you.' [my italics] Given Eliot's need for something clearly readable as Jewish, it is unsurprising that he should resort to stereotype—and then, as a writer who does not deal in stereotypes, reject it.

There is another related reason. 'Dirge' is also a parody of Ariel's song in *The Tempest*. It is one of several ironic contrasts with the past. Ariel's song is well known. To make a contrast with the present, Eliot needed something equally recognisable in the present. Unwisely, he chose a Jewish stereotype. And then, wisely, suppressed the poem. Why? Ezra Pound, an overt anti-Semite, thought it 'doubtful'—presumably on poetic grounds.[11] But it may be that, because the poem is coarsely reliant on caricature, its stereotyping is dangerously coterminous with anti-Semitism—and that the poem seemed dangerously so to Eliot, who therefore sacrificed it rather than risk charges of anti-Semitism. We cannot know.

There is something else crucial that we cannot know. We cannot know who is speaking 'Dirge'—since it is part of a dramatic poem, in which, as I have already explained, the one voice we do not hear is that of Eliot. Because 'Dirge' has not been allotted a place in the finished poem, everyone has assumed that 'Dirge' is spoken by Eliot. It is an unwarranted assumption.

In any case, it is intemperate and *inaccurate* of Julius to call it an anti-Semitic 'torture fantasy'—especially so when you contrast it with the authentic anti-Semitic torture fantasies supplied by Julius for the purpose of incriminating comparison. The manner of Bleistein's death is dictated by literary considerations—the parody—not by a determination to mock Jewish 'stateless transience'. As a misreading, this is as fatuous as Julius finding 'The Love Song of J. Alfred Prufrock' misogynist.

7. Eliot's Pro-Semitism

Suppose, however, that when all the evidence is in, posterity convicts Eliot of anti-Semitism. What then? It could be the case. Julius wants to censure, not censor. But my own instinct is to mitigate. If Eliot turns out, in his correspondence, say, to be anti-Semitic, it will not be simple. And I adduce three pieces of evidence, here, of Eliot's pro-Semitism. The first is the attack on the Blackshirts in *The Rock*—an attack that is specifically centred on their anti-Semitism. Here is the relevant quotation:

BLACKSHIRTS:

Your vesture, your gesture, your speech and your face,
Proclaim your extraction from Jewish race.
We have our own prophets, who're ready to speak
For a week and a day and a day and a week.
This being the case, we must firmly refuse
To descend to palaver with anthropoid Jews.

Obviously, this passage presents no difficulty for my case. But it is an embarrassment for Julius. To any unprejudiced reader, the passage is hostile to the Blackshirts because they are contemporary examples of anti-Semitic hatred. Julius equivocates: on page 106 of his book, he concedes that here 'anti-Semitism of a kind is repudiated expressly'. Note the reservation: 'of a kind'. Ninety pages later, Julius's argument shifts: 'the rejection of the Blackshirts' anti-Semitism is a rejection of anti-Christian paganism . . . It is not a plea for modern Jewry, it is an endorsement of Christianity'.

My second piece of evidence is Eliot's sympathetic account of the persecution of the Jews in the Diaspora, in 'A Song for Simeon':

Who shall remember my house, where shall live my children's
                                  children
When the time of sorrow is come?
They will take to the goat's path, and the fox's home,
Fleeing from the foreign faces and the foreign swords.

Julius knows that this presents a difficulty for his thesis, and he tries to answer it without properly alerting his reader. The crucial question is this: *when is* 'the time of sorrow'? Julius answers: 'not the moment of the dispersion of the Jews but that of the trials of

Christ, and of the early Christians.' I think the phrase 'my children's children' means 'posterity', but at the very least it means two generations. Even if taken literally, then, the phrase 'my children's children' is hardly synchronous with Christ's trial and crucifixion. But obviously the phrase is employed metaphorically for a posterity persecuted by 'foreign swords' and 'foreign faces'. Pogroms, in fact.

8. Charles Maurras

In the *London Review of Books* (31 August 1989), A. V. C. Schmidt long ago disposed of Erik Svarny's contention that 'Eliot did not repudiate Maurras's anti-Semitism'. Schmidt quoted Eliot's contribution to the *Christian News-Letter* of 3 September 1941, which condemned anti-Semitic policies being introduced in Vichy France:

> What gives us the gravest anxiety, is the statement [in the *Times* article cited] that 'Jews have been given a special status, based on the laws of Nuremberg, which makes their condition little better than that of bondsmen'. Anti-Semitism there has always been, among the parties of the extreme right: but it was a very different thing, as a symptom of the disorder of French society and politics for the last hundred and fifty years, from what it is when it takes place as a principle of reconstruction ... *we can only hope that there has been, or that there will be, some organised protest against such injustice* [my italics], by the French ecclesiastical hierarchy: unless we are also optimistic enough to hope that these measures are only taken under the strongest pressure from Germany, and that no French government, once that government was master in its own house, would enforce such measures or keep them on its statutes.

Schmidt concluded irrefutably that if Eliot repudiated anti-Semitism, 'in doing so by logical requirement [he] repudiated the anti-Semitism of Charles Maurras'. Nothing could be plainer than Eliot's explicit recognition of the fundamental injustice of anti-Semitism. Julius will have none of it. He massages the passage perversely and prejudicially like a tyro Deconstructionist until he can conclude *from this evidence* that 'Eliot had the imagination of an anti-Semite in the highest degree. He was alive to anti-Semitism's resources, insensitive to Jewish pain'. Eliot: 'we can only hope that there has been . . . some organised protest against such injustice.' When Julius weighs the evidence, it's as well to solicit a second opinion from a weights and measures inspector. The 'fluid' ounce takes on a changed semantic penumbra.[12]

Perhaps Eliot's correspondence will tell a different tale. As it may in the case of Charles Maurras, the anti-Semitic leader of Action Française, who was convicted of collaboration and treason after the war and whose views, some of them at least, Eliot found in 1955 'exasperating' and 'deplorable'. Which views we do not precisely know, since Eliot does not absolutely repudiate Maurras. Some Maurras's ideas he still finds 'sound and strong'. The Eliot scholar Ronald Schuchard told me a research student had written to the Maurras family and had been sent copies of Eliot's side of the correspondence. Letters exist, then, and will be published in due course. Until then, we must be patient and work with the evidence we have. For now, let us bear in mind Montgomery Belgion's clearly demarcated admiration for, and disavowal of, Maurras. And, of course, Eliot's condemnation of anti-Semitism in 1941: 'we can only hope that there has been, or that there will be, some organised protest against such injustice'.

The most obvious attraction of Maurras for Eliot is literary. He was one of several bickering French critics who espoused classicism as against romanticism—that is, the superiority of sense over sensibility, of reason over emotion. In 1930, Eliot commissioned for Faber a history of these intellectual tendencies, *Tradition and Barbarism*, by P. Mansell Jones, a French scholar from Cardiff. Jones's title tells us how much the movement had in common with Arnoldian precepts—Culture and Anarchy, obviously, but also Arnold's opposition of Attic to Asiatic. Maurras was one way Eliot could agree with Arnold without acknowledging his awkward father figure. In essence, these French thinkers, Charles Maurras, Julien Benda, Pierre Lasserre, were opposed to the exaggeration of emotion; their rallying cry was that, since Rousseau, literature was effeminate, and it overvalued the individual personality, originality, and excessive emotion.

Belphégor will serve as an exemplary classicist text. Its epigraph is from Bossuet: 'Is then the charm of feeling so great?'[13] In it, Julien Benda argues that French culture has become emotionally self-indulgent. He attributes this decadence partly to the influence of women. Menand thinks *Belphégor* is misogynist. If it is, it is because it uses 'the female temperament' as a synecdoche for emotional incontinence. For Benda, emotional incontinence wasn't inevitable in women: he praises 'the subtle distinctions' of Madame de Coligny and Madame de Grignan, the loss of whose 'dialectical power in French society' he laments. He cites, too, Madame de Staal-Delaunay's praise of the Duchess of Maine for lucidity and a quality of mind that has now vanished from society.

Benda knows that emotional decadence is often blamed on the Jews. How could he not? He was a Jew. This was the time of Dreyfus. In part II of *Belphégor*, he strategically defuses this anti-

Semitism by dividing the Jewish race into two symbolic types. He admits the bad influence of a certain kind of Jew—the sensualist who, in the Old Testament, worshipped the pagan god, Bal-Péor. (Hence Benda's title.) Lest we are tempted to attribute anti-Semitism to the Jewish and Dreyfusard Benda, it is important to point out that, for him, another kind of Jew represents the antidote to the emotionally self-indulgent. This is 'the severe, moralistic Jew', the Spinoza type—the rationalist, the thinker—who, in the Bible, worships not Bal-Péor but Jehovah. Benda then points out that anti-Semitic and non-Semitic groups equally espouse this ruinous, emotional aesthetic. His clever, implicit inference is that, therefore, you can't blame the Jews.

Eliot admired *Belphégor* very much. It is the template for *After Strange Gods*, Eliot's 'Primer of Modern Heresy', whose title and subtitle refer us to those Israelites in the Old Testament who worshipped pagan gods—like Bal-Péor. In *After Strange Gods*, the contest is between external authority and rampant individualism, between a moral literature and emotion for emotion's sake—between, as it were, Jehovah and Bal-Péor. These are the classicist fundamentals.

Mansell Jones is quite clear that within the movement there were disagreements, shades of opinion; Benda, for instance, accused Maurras of 'the Romanticism of Reason'. Exactly where Eliot stood on every detail isn't clear. The participants were diverse, and Eliot, for example, praised Benda's *Belphégor* but expressed reservations about his *Trahison des clercs*.

Yet these fundamental, unemotional classicist ideas lie behind Flaubert's great treatment of Emma Bovary's death by arsenic poisoning. She thinks, 'I shall go to sleep, and it will all be over.' Which is how it might be in conventional literature—romantic literature, feminine literature, George Eliot's 'Silly Novels by Lady Novelists'. *Madame Bovary* is, among other things, a reading list of 'the latest volumes of smooth twaddle', as Henry James puts it. Emma Bovary has read the lot. But Flaubert gives us the poisoning as it would be: prolonged, painful, retching, vomiting blood, tasting ink, brown spots on the body, dilated pupils, convulsions, a million miles from romantic preconceptions, in fact. Eliot, like Joyce (another writer of classical temper), chose the Flaubertian, Maurrasian way. Whether this entailed the assumption of Maurras's anti-Semitism also we cannot say as yet. It does not necessarily follow.

To these particular arguments I would like to add a more general plea of mitigation. Milan Kundera, in *Testaments Betrayed*, one of the century's great and wise books, says that man is not in the dark, but in a fog.

> He sees fifty yards ahead of him, he can clearly make out the features of his interlocutor, can take pleasure in the beauty of the trees that line the path, and can even observe what is happening close by and react. Man proceeds in the fog. But when he looks back to judge the people of the past, he sees no fog on their path . . . their path looks perfectly clear to him, good visibility all the way. Looking back, he sees the patch, he sees the people proceeding, he sees their mistakes, but not the fog.

What a measured and just rebuke to self-righteousness this is. If there prove to be unequivocal anti-Semitic elements in the record left by Eliot, we should bear this rebuke in mind.

Two Free Translations
by Craig Raine of
'Lune de Miel' and
'Dans le Restaurant'

HONEYMOON

They have seen the low countries, they will return to the high
    ground—
Terre Haute in Vigo County, Indiana;
But now it's a hot night, and here they are at Ravenna,
Limp between the sheets, home of two hundred or so bedbugs;
Summer sweat and a powerful pong of bitch.
They lie on their backs, keeping their knees apart;
Four feeble limbs muscular with bites.
They lift up the sheet to scratch more intensely.
Less than a league from here, St Apollinaire
En classe, basilica known to amateurs
For its acanthine capitals which the wind whirls around.

They are going to take the 8 a.m. train
To prolong their miseries from Padua to Milan,

Where the Last Supper is—and a reasonably priced restaurant.
He thinks about tipping and tots up his accounts.
They will have seen Switzerland and crossed France.
And St Apollinaire, stiff and ascetic,
An old disused god factory,
Still hoards in its worn stones
The sharp silhouette of its Byzantine build.

IN THE RESTAURANT

The down-at-heel waiter with nothing to do
Except scratch his fingers and lean on my shoulder:
'In my neck of the woods the weather will be rainy,
windy, boiling hot, rainy;
it's what they call weather for washing up the beggars.'
(Gossip, dribbler, with a rounded rump,
I beg you, at least, not to gob in my soup.)
'Drenched willows, buds on the brambles—
It was there, in a shower, that we took shelter.
I was seven; she was smaller.
She was soaked to her skin. I gave her primroses.'
I totted up the stains on his waistcoat. They came to a total of
    thirty-eight.
'I tickled her to make her laugh.

I experienced a moment of power and delirium.'

All the same, you dirty old man, at that age . . .
'Sir, fate is hard. Then a big dog came along, pawing us.
I was afraid, I stopped half way.
What a shame.'

But still, you have your vulture!
Go and get the grime out of the wrinkles in your face;
Take my fork, and give your skull a good clean out.
How dare you have experiences like me?
Here, ten sous, to go to the public baths.

Phlebas the Phoenician, fifteen days drowned,
Forgot the cry of seagulls and the Cornish swell,
Profit and loss and the freight of tin:
The undertow carried him far away,
Passing the stages of his previous life.
Imagine it. Like this. A dismal destiny.
All the same. Once a beautiful man, a tall man.

Appendix 3

AN ELIOT CHRONOLOGY

1888 26 September: Thomas Stearns Eliot born in St. Louis, Missouri, the youngest of six children.

1906 October: Enters Harvard University.

1910 July and August: Fair copies his poetry into a notebook entitled *Inventions of the March Hare.*

September: Begins a year of study at the Sorbonne in Paris.

1911 Attends Bergson's lectures at the Collège de France.

July and August: Travels to Italy and Munich, finishes final version of 'The Love Song of J. Alfred Prufrock'. He is twenty-three.

September: Returns to Harvard to do a doctorate in philosophy. Enrols in Charles Lanman's Indic philology course, studies Sanskrit and Pali. J. H. Woods teaches him Indian philosophy. (As TSE records in *After Strange Gods* and *Notes towards the Definition of Culture.*)

1913 Withdraws from the Sanskrit course.

1914 January: Awarded a Sheldon Travelling Scholarship to go to Oxford University.

June: Leaves Harvard for Europe.

July: At University of Marburg in Germany.

August: World War One begins.

22 September: Eliot visits Ezra Pound in Kensington.

October: At Merton College, Oxford to work on F. H. Bradley.

1915 26 June: Marries Vivien Haigh-Wood.

July: Returns to the United States. Eliot's father discontinues his allowance.

10 September: Writes to his father about money worries, and gives reasons for his decision to stay in England.

1916 February: Completes doctoral thesis.

September: Begins a lecture series, for extension courses, on modern French and English literature at Oxford and in London.

1917 19 March: Starts work at Lloyds Bank.

6 April: United States enters the war; Eliot turned down by U.S. Navy because of congenital hernia.

June: Appointed assistant editor of *The Egoist. Prufrock and Other Observations* published by the Egoist Press.

1918 September: Gives first of eighteen lectures on Elizabethan literature at a school in Sydenham, in southeast London.

1919 8 January: Eliot's father dies.

29 March: Eliot turns down Middleton Murry's offer of assistant editorship at the *Athenaeum*.

1920 February: Alfred A. Knopf in New York publishes *Poems by T. S. Eliot*.

August: Eliot holidays in France with Wyndham Lewis; meets James Joyce in Paris.

November: *The Sacred Wood* is published.

1921 April: Eliot attends Ballets Russes with his brother Henry, who is on a visit with their mother. TSE cheers Stravinsky's *Le Sacre du Printemps*.

November: Leaves for Lausanne for health reasons.

December: Returns to London via Paris; shows Pound *The Waste Land*, which Pound promptly edits to 433 lines.

1922 September: *The Dial* agrees to publish *The Waste Land* and to give TSE the annual award of $2,000.

October: Eliot edits his first issue of *The Criterion*, which includes first publication of *The Waste Land*. He is thirty-three.

November: *The Waste Land* published in *The Dial*.

December: Boni & Liveright publish *The Waste Land* in book form.

1923 September: Hogarth Press issues first British publication of *The Waste Land*.

1924 Vivien Eliot seriously ill in the winter months.

1925   March: *The Hollow Men* published, without later part III.

July: *The Criterion* ceases publication until January 1926.

November: Eliot leaves the bank and joins the publishing firm of Faber and Gwyer (later Faber and Faber). Faber publishes *Poems 1909–1925*.

1926   January to March: Eliot delivers the Clark lectures at Cambridge.

January: *The New Criterion* appears then ceases publication until May, when it reappears as *The Monthly Criterion*. Monthly editions follow until March 1928.

1927   29 June: Eliot received into the Church of England. His baptism followed by confirmation on 30 June.

2 November: Eliot becomes a naturalised British citizen.

1928   June to January 1939: *The Criterion* reverts to being a quarterly.

20 November: In *For Lancelot Andrewes*, Eliot defines himself as 'classicist in literature, royalist in politics and Anglo-Catholic in religion'.

1929   10 September: Eliot's mother dies.

1930   24 April: *Ash-Wednesday* published.

May: *Anabasis*, Eliot's translation of St. John Perse published.

1932   Autumn: Eliot decides to accept the invitation to give the Charles Eliot Norton lectures at Harvard.

September: *Selected Essays* published.

4 November: Eliot gives first Harvard lecture; series concludes 31 March 1933.

December: *Sweeney Agonistes* published.

1933 January: Eliot gives Turnbull lectures at Johns Hopkins University.

February: Instructs his lawyers to act in his separation from Vivien.

June: Returns to England, avoiding his wife.

Autumn: Returns to University of Virginia to deliver the Page-Barbour lectures, which are published in 1934 as *After Strange Gods*.

Winter: Moves to clergy house of St. Stephen's Church. Lives there for next five years.

1934 February: publication of *After Strange Gods*.

May: *The Rock* opens at Sadlers Wells Theatre in London.

1935 June: *Murder in the Cathedral* first performed in the Chapter House of Canterbury Cathedral.

1936 April: *Collected Poems 1909–1935* published, includes the first publication of *Burnt Norton*.

1938 August: Vivien Eliot committed to a mental hospital by her brother.

1939 January: Last issue of *The Criterion* published.

March: Eliot gives three lectures at Corpus Christi College, Cambridge; they become *The Idea of a Christian Society*.

The Family Reunion opens at the Westminster Theatre in London.

October: *Old Possum's Book of Practical Cats* is published.

1940 March: *New English Weekly* publishes *East Coker.*

September: Faber publishes *East Coker* in pamphlet form.

1941 20 February: Faber publishes *Burnt Norton* in pamphlet form.

27 February: *New English Weekly* publishes *The Dry Salvages.*

4 September: Faber publishes *The Dry Salvages.*

1942 15 October: *New English Weekly* publishes *Little Gidding.*

1 December: Faber publishes *Little Gidding* in the usual pamphlet form.

1943 11 May: *Four Quartets* published together in the United States for first time.

1944 31 October: Faber publishes *Four Quartets.*

1945 December: Eliot makes first visit to the United States in thirteen years. Visits the incarcerated Ezra Pound at St. Elizabeth's; Pound had been arrested on charges of treason in May for making pro-Fascist broadcasts on Rome radio during the war.

1946 Eliot moves in to John Hayward's Cheyne Walk flat and lives there until his second marriage, to Valerie Fletcher, in January 1957.

1947 23 January: Vivien, Eliot's first wife, dies in a private mental hospital in Finsbury Park, London.

1948 January: Eliot awarded the Order of Merit.

July: Penguin publishes *Selected Poems* in a printing of 50,000.

5 November: Faber publishes *Notes towards the Definition of Culture*.

10 December: Eliot receives Nobel Prize.

1949   22 August: *The Cocktail Party* opens at the Lyceum Theatre, Edinburgh.

Autumn: Eliot on six-week lecture tour in Germany with Arnold Toynbee, the historian.

1950   21 January: *The Cocktail Party* opens in New York City.

9 March: Faber publishes *The Cocktail Party*.

October and November: Eliot delivers four lectures on education at the University of Chicago.

December: Suffers a mild heart attack.

1952   29 November: Faber publishes *Complete Poems and Plays (1909–1950)*.

1953   March: Penguin publishes Eliot's *Selected Prose* (chosen by John Hayward) in a printing of 40,000.

25 August: *The Confidential Clerk* opens at the Lyceum Theatre, Edinburgh.

1954   April: Eliot has a serious heart attack.

1955   5 May: Receives the Hanseatic Goethe Award in Hamburg and lectures on 'Goethe As the Sage'.

1956   19 April: Sails to the United States for six-week visit.

12 June: Suffers attack of tachycardia on voyage back; rushed to hospital.

1957 10 January: Marries Valerie Fletcher, who has been his secretary since 1950.

13 September: *On Poetry and Poets* published and dedicated to Valerie Eliot.

1958 25 August: *The Elder Statesman* produced at Edinburgh festival.

26 September: Eliot turns seventy.

1962 Towards the end of the year, Eliot dangerously ill and spends five weeks in London's Brompton Hospital.

1965 4 January: Eliot dies in London.

NOTES

CHAPTER 1

1. Latin: a little soul, life.
2. I'm reminded of *Brideshead Revisited* when Ryder evokes the secondhand 'experience' of revolution, immediate yet twice-removed: 'one had read it in the papers, seen it in the films, heard it at café tables again and again for six or seven years, till it had become part of one's experience, like the mud of Flanders and the flies of Mesopotamia.'
3. You could argue, however, that Gerontion is aggrandising and melodramatising his predicament by using the word 'inquisition' where 'self-doubt' or 'self-questioning' would be more accurate. He is glamorising an act of timidity. Compare: 'Is not Cyrano exactly in this position of contemplating himself as a romantic, a dramatic figure' ('"Rhetoric" and Poetic Drama'). Or, Eliot on Othello's final speech: 'What Othello seems to me to be doing in making this speech is *cheering himself up*. He is endeavouring to escape reality, he has ceased to think about Desdemona, and is thinking about himself' ('Shakespeare and the Stoicism of Seneca').
4. A variant on the more conventionally 'trembling' star and Eliot's reminiscence of Tennyson's 'stars that shudder over me' in 'The Coming of Arthur' from *The Idylls of the King*.
5. Every reader senses a link back to 'Christ the tiger'—especially since Eliot leaves that earlier line unpunctuated, as if the thought would be completed later. But I think this is wrong. In fact, Eliot's link back is illusory, there only to show us another disrupted sequence in a poem in which sequence is reliably unreliable: 'Unnatural vices / Are fathered by our heroism.' We go from 'Christ the tiger' to a different kind of tiger.
6. Quoted by Eliot in 'Eeldrop and Appleplex' (*The Little Review*, May and September 1917), where Eeldrop credits the words to an old flame, Edith, a.k.a. 'Scheherezade', a romantic type with a 'passion for experience'.
7. I think Eliot is generalising his contrast between Webster and Donne and 'our lot', but it is conceivable that, by 'our lot', he means modern *writers*.
8. They are exactly like the eponymous protagonist of Kipling's poem 'Tomlinson', whose person and whose moral vapidity is rejected equally by heaven and by hell: '"Do you think I would waste my good pit-coal on the hide of a brain-sick fool?"' says the Devil.
9. No wonder, given his temperament, Eliot wrote, in a footnote to his essay 'Baudelaire in Our Time' (1928): 'Of course Mr Shaw and Mr Wells are also much occupied with religion and *Ersatz-Religion*. But they are concerned with the spirit, not the letter. And the spirit killeth, but the letter giveth life.'
10. 'For now, a vision came before him, as constant and more terrible than that from which he had escaped. Those widely staring eyes, so lustreless and so glassy, that he had better borne to see them than think upon them, appeared in the midst of the darkness; light in themselves, but giving light to nothing. There were but two, but they were everywhere.' Quoting *Oliver Twist*, however, shows how much less specific Eliot is— his speaker being constitutionally evasive.

11. Greek: impassable path (and therefore an obstacle to completion).
12. Section IV of *Ash-Wednesday* ends 'And after this our exile'—where the secular exile of Cavalcanti is clearly transposed to the theological. Exile here is an exile from God, which is soon to be over. Eliot has in mind the prayer 'Salve Regina': 'And, after this our exile, show unto us the blessed fruit of thy womb, Jesus.'
13. The idea that God is unknowable except by revelation, and that all things earthly make God more unknowable by corruption. The mystic, therefore, empties his mind of all he knows and of every created thing and idea so as to be unimpeded in the search for God.
14. He is like a man seeing a Token—'a wraith of the living', according to Kipling in 'The Wish House'. In this case, it is a self-haunting. Compare Kipling's 'At the End of the Passage': 'the first thing he saw standing in the verandah was the figure of himself.'
15. My *Chambers Twentieth Century Dictionary* gives '*Taxus baccata* (in Europe long planted in graveyards)'. (Compare Tennyson's *In Memoriam*: 'Old yew, which graspest at the stones / That name the underlying dead.')
16. Compare—and weigh—Eliot's quotation from Bradley's *The Principles of Logic*: 'That the glory of this world in the end is appearance leaves the world more glorious, if we feel it is a show of some fuller splendour.'
17. The sentiment, 'Teach us to care and not to care', is reminiscent of Kipling's 'The Second Voyage', another poem of middle age: 'Yet, caring so, not overmuch we care, / To brace and trim for every foolish blast.'
18. Compare Ricks's *T. S. Eliot and Prejudice* (1988), page 231. We share an orientation but differ in emphasis and detail.
19. The poem's epigraph refers us to Seneca's *Hercules Furens* at the moment when Hercules recovers from the madness that has caused him to kill his wife and children. Pericles is in a similar moment of awakening, of apprising, of reentry. Otherwise, the Seneca scenario of slaughter is irrelevant to Eliot's poem.
20. There is a hint of senility in Pericles's initially distracted, wandering speech in act 5—and it is no surprise that Dickens modelled William Dorrit on Pericles, down to a shared 'Hum! Ha!' Dorrit, of course, ends with a wandering mind.
21. But at the actual moment of death, Tolstoy wants to make a moral point, not a phenomenological one.

CHAPTER 2

1. The '"Jug Jug" to dirty ears' of 'A Game of Chess' isn't specific to the nightingale, but is a conventional onomatopoeic representation in Elizabethan poetry of bird song in general. See 'Spring Song' in Nashe's 'Summer's Last Will and Testament', which has *all* the bird sounds.
2. It is often said, by those who want to portray Eliot as a political reactionary, that the very definition apes Albert Thibaudet's footnote in *Nouvelle Revue Française* (March 1914), which describes Maurras's traditions as 'classique, catholique, monarchique'. Echoes, certainly. Apes, possibly—but not necessarily. Perhaps Eliot had Goethe in mind. Goethe (6 January 1813) wrote to Jacobi that he was a polytheist in poetry, a pantheist in science, and a monotheist in ethics: 'als Dichter und Künstler bin ich Polytheist, Pantheist hingegen als Naturforscher, und eins so entschieden als das andre.' And in *Goethes Gespräche*, we find Dorothea von Schlegel writing to her sons (28 November 1817) that Goethe had described himself as an atheist in science and philosophy, a pagan in art, and a Christian by emotional inclination: 'Goethe hat einem Durchreisenden offenbart, er sei in der Naturkunde und Philosophie ein Atheist, im der Kunst ein / Heide und dem Gefühl nach ein Christ!'
3. The other Benda books then unknown to Eliot include a Dreyfusard commentary on the Dreyfus affair in *La Revue Blanche* in 1898, ten articles, which became the book

Dialogues à Byzance, a repudiation of French anti-Semitism, published in 1900 and subsequently praised by Eliot; a novel *L'Ordination* (1912); and two attacks on Bergson, *Le Bergsonisme* (1912) and *Sur le succès du Bergsonisme* (1917). *Belphégor* was published in 1918.

4. Later, in 'The Humanism of Irving Babbitt' (1928), Eliot was to use Benda's argument against Maurras, against Benda himself: 'M. Julien Benda . . . has a romantic view of critical detachment which limits his interest.'

5. Even though Flaubert said *Madame Bovary* was written against the realist novel, he is nevertheless the first realist: his negative comment referred to the painter Courbet, and the novelists Edmond Duranty and Champfleury, who were associated with Courbet as practitioners of what might be called the inventory school of realism. I owe this point to Adam Thirlwell.

6. Joyce's analogy is stolen, strangely enough, from Wilde's *The Picture of Dorian Gray*: Lord Henry 'had been always enthralled by the methods of natural sciences, but the ordinary subject matter of that science had seemed to him trivial and of no import. So he had begun by vivisecting himself, as he had ended by vivisecting others.'

7. In his 1926 Clark lectures and the recast version in his 1933 Turnbull lectures, Eliot *did* write about Laforgue, though it was not until 1993 that the texts were published in *The Varieties of Metaphysical Poetry* (edited by Ronald Schuchard). In both, Eliot's version of Laforgue is an oddly staid, subdued figure steeped in 'Kant, Schopenhauer and Hartmann' and preoccupied with the idea that 'every feeling should have its emotional equivalent, its philosophical justification, and that every idea should have its emotional equivalent, its sentimental justification'. He is, in a word, a metaphysical writer, awkwardly coopted into Eliot's debate about the dissociation of sensibility— and it is only at the last minute that we learn that a sprightlier Laforgue exists, one who *entertains* philosophical ideas and has a *cool, detached* attitude to his feelings.

8. Obviously, I've excluded *Poems Written in Early Youth*, which includes three Laforguean exercises.

9. In his essay on Stendhal, Valéry remarks of the confessional style: 'After all, it must be rather fun, by the mere fact of unbuttoning one's fly, to give oneself and other people the impression of discovering America.'

10. First formulated by Stephen Medcalf in *T. S. Eliot at the Turn of the Century*, edited by Marianne Thormählen (Lund University Press, 1994).

11. Not for the first time, however. Shakespeare's 'Venus and Adonis' is another instance.

12. Or compare chapter 54 of *Pride and Prejudice*, in which Elizabeth Bennet is on tenterhooks about Darcy's intentions, hoping for a renewal of his attentions, but tied to the task of pouring coffee for the general company.

13. Eliot could have quoted Pater's conclusion to *The Renaissance*: 'Experience, already reduced to a group of impressions, is ringed round for each one of us by that thick wall of personality through which no real voice has ever pierced its way to us, or from us to that which we can only conjecture to be without. Every one of these impressions is the impression of the individual in his isolation, each mind keeping as a solitary prisoner its own dream of the world.'

14. *Appearance and Reality*, chapter 23, 'Body and Soul', page 304.

15. *Ibid.*, page 317.

CHAPTER 3

1. The 'handful of dust' is also thought to be a reference to the Sibyl of Cumae's fate (evoked in Eliot's epigraph) and to Donne's meditation 4 in *Devotions upon Emergent Occasions* (1624).

2. Eliot in '*Ulysses*, Order and Myth' in the *Dial* 1923.

3. In Greek, it means 'actor'.

4. Eliot died nine years later in 1965. But he had written off, in a wry, humorous paragraph, the life's work of Grover Smith, a leading Eliot scholar, with a crucial investment in Tarot and Grail. Grover Smith began in 1950 with *The Poems of T. S. Eliot 1909—1928: A Study in Symbols and Sources*. This was engrossed and superseded by *T. S. Eliot's Poetry and Plays: A Study in Sources and Meaning* (1956). After several impressions, a second edition appeared in 1974. In his preface, Grover Smith noted: 'There is no compassion in Eliot's poetry when, occasionally, Vivienne figures in it: there is profuse testimony to Eliot's misery, none to hers. This fact horrifies and repels me.' The tart distaste here and the petulance passim is all-too-human testimony to the pronounced leeward list of his critical study—comprehensively holed below the waterline.

5. Neither Frazer nor Jessie L. Weston is an influential figure in current Grail scholarship.

6. In both Chrétien de Troyes's *Perceval—Conté de Graal* and Wolfram von Eschenbach's *Parzifal*, it is Parsifal (Percival) who finds the Grail. In Malory, Perceval, Galahad, and Bors take Eucharist from Christ and take the Grail to Sarras.

7. Compare the tarnished cupids in *A Tale of Two Cities*, chapter 4: 'The likeness passed away, like a breath along the surface of a gaunt pier-glass behind her, on the frame of which, a hospital procession of negro cupids, several headless and all crippled, were offering black baskets of Dead Sea fruit to black divinities of the feminine gender.'

8. In Eliot's June 1921 'London Letter' in *The Dial*, he regrets the threatened demolition of St. Mary Woolnoth and St. Magnus Martyr—which adds another, more literal interpretation to the phrase, 'unreal city'.

9. In a letter to William Alfred (22 September 1972) Robert Lowell makes the same equation between New England and the desert: 'I love England; often I wish it were entirely inhabited by Americans. Couldn't we give England New England in exchange. Swamps would be drained, slums and wasteland redeemed—as T S Eliot would have desired.'

CHAPTER 4

1. 'Much like us' in another sense, too. The idea of the simultaneity of all time is common early in the Christian philosophical tradition. Boethius's *De Consolatione Philosophiae* book 5, prose 6 tells us that knowledge is relative. Its scope depends on the individual. God's knowledge is therefore superior to human knowledge: 'God hath always an everlasting and present state, His knowledge also surpassing all notions of time, remaineth in the simplicity of His presence, and comprehending the infinite spaces of that which is past and to come, considereth all things in His simple knowledge as though they were now in doing.' It is part of the unavoidable debate about human free will in the context of divine omniscience.

2. In the aptly titled *Transparent Things*, the ghosts of dead characters narrate. Nabokov's story, 'The Vane Sisters', describes the hereafter as 'a silent solarium of immortal souls (spliced with mortal antecedents) whose main recreation consisted of periodical hoverings over the dear quick'.

3. A deliberately jarring, unpoetic neologism at the time of writing *East Coker*.

4. *Ostranenie* (a Russian neologism coined by Viktor Shklovsky): making strange, defamiliarising.

5. From *The Boke of the Governour*, book 1, chapter 21.

6. The seasonal mélange in section II of *East Coker* is followed by the destruction of planetary harmony and images of apocalypse, a larger confusion of a larger order, concluding in the paradox of 'destructive fire' creating 'the ice-cap'.

7. Eliot's source here is perhaps a reminiscence of Emma Bovary's death from arsenic poisoning: 'her pulse slid between the fingers like a taut wire, like a harp-string about to snap.'

8. 'Le Directeur' and 'Mélange Adultère de Tout' both send up the lyric by wedding prosaic content to intense rhyming. 'Le directeur / Conservateur / Du Spectateur / Empeste la brise. / Les actionnaires / Réactionnaires / Du Spectateur / Conservateur' makes a mockery of Verlaine's 'Les sanglots longs / Des violons / De l'automne / Blessent mon coeur / D'une langeur / Monotone.' ('Chanson d'Automne')

CHAPTER 5

1. A quarter of a century earlier, in the fifth of his Clark lectures at Cambridge in 1926, Eliot addressed the same idea in a slightly different formulation. He is talking about the Elizabethan dramatist, Chapman: 'I have always been impressed . . . by the sense of a "double world" in the tragedies of Chapman, [and] which made me compare him to Dostoevski. Here and there the actors in his drama appear as if following another train of thought, listening to other voices, feeling with other senses; and acting out another scene than that visible upon the stage.' The buried life is a hardy, lifelong, animating intuition for Eliot. I say 'intuition' because, obviously, the hypothesis lends itself neither to proof nor to falsification. Adam Thirlwell drew my attention to this quotation.

2. Emrys Jones's marvellous essay, '*Murder in the Cathedral* at Stratford' (in *T. S. Eliot at the Turn of the Century*, edited by Marianne Thormählen, Lund University Press) is a meticulous and electrifying account of Stephen Pimlott's 1993 production. Jones's argument, beautifully illustrated and sustained, is that Eliot's play *is* highly dramatic— and that the drama, though helped by historical authenticity of the events staged and significantly enriched by directorial additions, is clearer because its religious appeal is now more or less defunct. Clearly, the production worked, because it still works in Emrys Jones's bravura retelling. But the question is, does the *play* work?

CHAPTER 6

1. 'However, he didn't mind thinking that if Cissy should prove all that was likely enough their having a subject in common couldn't but practically conduce; though the moral of it all amounted rather to a portent, the one that Haughty, by the same token, had done least to reassure him against, of the extent to which the native jungle harboured the female specimen and to which its ostensible cover, the vast level of mixed growths stirred waveringly in whatever breeze, was apt to be identifiable but as an agitation of the latest redundant thing in ladies' hats.'

2. There is a sense, however, in which the speech *is* a press release—though not in the way Eliot means. Raphael reports Satan's speech to Adam and Eve, just as Raphael reports God's speech. You could argue that God's clear syntax and Satan's turbid, troubled syntax are examples of publicity management by Raphael. Beginning as both speeches do with 'Thrones, Dominations, Virtues, Powers', they ask to be compared and contrasted.

3. For the purpose of exposition, I 'accept' Eliot's reading of Hamlet's psychology: 'Hamlet (the man) is dominated by an emotion which is inexpressible, because it is in *excess* of the facts as they appear.' Actually, one might mount a convincing challenge by quoting Rosencrantz in Stoppard's *Rosencrantz and Guildenstern Are Dead*: 'To sum up: your father, whom you love, dies, you are his heir, you come back to find that hardly was his corpse cold before his young brother popped on to his throne and into his sheets, thereby offending both legal and natural practice. Now why exactly are you behaving in this extraordinary manner?'

4. Though Eliot is widely credited with the formulation, in 'Tradition and the Individual Talent', of the doctrine of impersonality in art, the idea is in the air. Proust's *Contre Sainte-Beuve*: 'a book is the product of a different self from the one we manifest in our habits, in society, in our vices. If we mean to try to understand this self it is only in our

inmost depths, by endeavouring to reconstruct it there, that the quest can be achieved.' Proust starts his argument against Sainte-Beuve with a position almost identical to Eliot's 'the more perfect the artist, the more completely separate in him will be the man who suffers and the mind which creates'. Henry James's 1893 story, 'The Private Life', is another illustration: in it, the writer Clare Vawdrey socialises while his doppelgänger writes in an upstairs room. The Proust shows that the creative self isn't the social self but a self in 'the inmost depths'—in other words, the buried life.

5. Dickens notices something similar when, in *A Tale of Two Cities*, he records the various expressions of those going to the guillotine, including 'some so heedful of their looks that they cast upon the multitude such glances as they have seen in theatres, and in pictures'.

Appendix 1

1. Eliot in 1956, quoted in *Affectionately, T. S. Eliot: The Story of a Friendship: 1947–1965* by William Turner Levy and Victor Scherle (1968). Eliot added: 'And they do not know [the slanderers], as you and I do, that in the eyes of the Church, to be anti-Semitic is a sin.'

2. Or, possibly, that it could not be answered in a letter. Witness the length of this appendix—unpublishable in the letters column of the *Times Literary Supplement*.

3. As the *London Review of Books* correspondent Daniel Adamski pointed out (20 June 1996), 'Raine is the only one to state that the review is "inadmissable evidence" if we cannot prove Eliot's authorship'.

4. *London Review of Books*, vol. 10, no. 9.

5. Eliot's deprecatory remark about 'fiercely self-conscious' cultures rules out the idea that he is considering separatism or ghettos. He is thinking about immigration—like many other people at the time. The history of U.S. immigration policy is relevant here. U.S. quotas can be seen as pragmatic attempts to avoid racial unrest. Nowadays, with the benefit of hindsight, they tend to be seen as racist. At the time, though, quotas had legal standing. Organised labour was against unrestricted immigration because the influx of cheap labour drove wages down. In 1882, the Chinese Exclusion Law excluded all Chinese immigrants; it was renewed indefinitely in 1902 and was not repealed until 1943. While the Homestead Acts (1862 and 1909) encouraged immigration from northern Europe, other measures discouraged immigration from southern Europe. In 1906, knowledge of English was made a basic requirement for naturalisation. In 1907, Japanese immigration was severely restricted through an understanding with Japan. Before 1920, however, there were no numerical restrictions on immigration. There were qualitative criteria. Not until 1917 was the literacy test made law, however. In 1921, the Temporary Quota Act, the first quantitative immigration law was adopted. It set temporary annual quotas according to national origin. In 1924, the Johnson-Reed National Origins Act, the first permanent immigration quota law was passed. Under this law immigration numbers were set to reflect the ethnic composition of the United States in 1920. Irish, Germans, and English, therefore, were favoured. The measure was designed to discriminate against Russian, Polish, and Italian immigrants. Asians were virtually excluded as a result of the Japanese Exclusion Act. In 1929, the annual quotas of the 1924 Act were made permanent.

6. Professor Fenton concluded his lecture by denouncing Eliot as a 'scoundrel'.

7. The argument I make is difficult for Anthony Julius. In his revised edition, he dismisses it as 'wrong'. First, we should bear in mind that neither he nor any other commentator identified the quotation. He pronounced without knowing the facts—which he now dismisses *as if he had known them all along*. Second, it is not *me*, but Eliot, who, by using the quotation, makes 'culture' and 'nation' analogous. It is beside the point, therefore, for Julius to insist so desperately on their difference.

8. See pages 45–46 for fuller exposition of this point.
9. This is a point Julius is now prepared to concede.
10. It is Julius's contention that *all* dramatic monologues 'have an autobiographical aspect, however small'. Is Browning, therefore, a jealous murderer—like his Duke of Ferrara, or Porphyria's lover? What—apart from imagination—does Iago or Regan owe to Shakespeare?
11. On 24 December 1921, Pound wrote to Eliot about *The Waste Land* manuscript in its edited form: 'One test is whether anything would be lacking if the last three [poems] were omitted. I don't think it would.' Valerie Eliot assumes, rightly, that one of these three was 'Dirge'.
12. It would be categorically perverse to read this passage as a repudiation of anti-Semitism as embodied in the Nuremberg laws and as an *endorsement* of prewar anti-Semitism. Eliot's distinction between the two is accurate, a matter of record. But saying extreme right wing anti-Semitism was 'a very different thing' does not strike a note of approval.
13. Boussuet's *Histoire des variations* is the great Catholic attack on Protestant individualism and proliferating sects.

INDEX

Note: Authors' literary works listed separately